Body & Soul

SUSAN MELTSNER, M.S.W.

MJF BOOKS

NEW YORK

Published by MJF Books
Fine Communications
Two Lincoln Square
60 West 66th Street
New York, NY 10023

ISBN 1-56731-114-8

Copyright © 1993 by Susan Meltsner

Manufactured in the United States of America

MJF Books and the MJF colophon are trademarks of Fine Creative Media, Inc.

10   9   8   7   6   5   4   3   2   1

Editor's Note

The Twelve Steps of AA are reprinted with permission of Alcoholics Anonymous World Services, Inc. Permission to reprint the Twelve Steps of Alcoholics Anonymous does not mean that Alcoholics Anonymous has reviewed or approved the contents of this publication, or that AA agrees with the views expressed herein. The views expressed herein are solely those of the author. AA is a program of recovery from alcoholism. Use of the Twelve Steps in connection with programs and activities that are patterned after AA, but which address other problems, does not imply otherwise.

Permission to use the Twelve Steps of Alcoholics Anonymous for adaptation granted to Overeaters Anonymous by AA World Services, Inc. The Twelve Steps of Overeaters Anonymous, as adapted, are reprinted here with the permission of Overeaters Anonymous, Inc. Permission to reprint OA's Twelve Steps does not mean that OA agrees with the views expressed herein.

All quotes and personal stories found in the anecdotes and examples in this book reflect the actual words and experiences of these real men and women. Unless otherwise noted, all names and identifying details have been changed in order to protect the subjects' anonymity. In some instances, the experiences of several people have been combined to form composite case studies. NO therapy or OA group member's actual words appear on these pages unless he or she agreed to be quoted.

Contents

CONTENTS

PART III
EMOTIONAL, SOCIAL, AND SPIRITUAL RECOVERY

PART IV
THE JOURNEY CONTINUES

Acknowledgments

While writing this book, I learned the true meaning of emotional support. I needed lots of it and received all I needed, thanks to Cindy Cannevari, Angela O'Reilly, David Townsend, Lori and Jeff Gregg, the "Blue Swan Sisters," and Dr. Sharon Kamm. I value and appreciate you all more than this brief acknowledgment can begin to convey.

I would also like to thank my agent, Ling Lucas; my acquisitions editor, Rebecca Post; my manuscript editor, Maureen Meyer; and Cathy Hemming, who took a chance on me as an unproven writer six years ago. Without you, this book wouldn't exist.

Finally, I'd like to dedicate this book to the hundreds of recovering compulsive eaters and bulimics whose paths have crossed mine. Your strength and courage have sustained and inspired me. I am eternally grateful to each and every one of you.

Introduction

Dear Reader,

If you're like most people who eat (or do anything else) compulsively, you don't care for surprises. Surprise parties are okay, and a surprise gift of diamonds or round-the-world cruise tickets is easy to take. But surprises and unknowns in any relationship or activity can be nerve-wracking. We prefer to know in advance what we're getting into, what could go wrong, and if our efforts will be worth the outcomes.

In the course of our everyday lives, we usually have to forge ahead without that information, but it isn't unreasonable to ask for it from an author, especially one who wants you to get the most out of her book. And I do. So let me answer some questions that may be rumbling around in your mind.

Is This Book for You?

It is if you . . .

- know in your heart that your relationship with food has been out of whack.
- acknowledge, even reluctantly, that too much of your time and energy has been devoted to thinking about what you ate, how you looked, how much you weighed, and how you could control or change those things (preferably overnight).
- see, even vaguely, that your attitudes and actions concerning these things have been adversely affecting your self-esteem, relationships, career, finances, and so on, or preventing you from leading a healthy, happy, full life.

1

- recognize that your problem cannot be solved through sheer willpower or by the latest quick-weight-loss plan.

If you are also actively involved in the Twelve Step program of Overeaters Anonymous (OA), in treatment with an eating disor· der specialist, or have abstained from your problematic behavior continuously for twenty-one days or more—that's terrific. I encourage all of these things. But they are not required for you to benefit from this book. You can benefit as long as *you are not totally in the dark about the nature and potential consequences of your eating or dieting behavior and not in denial about needing outside help to deal with it.*

I chose these particular—and admittedly broad—criteria for this book's audience because I wanted to give the greatest possible number of eating disorder sufferers the opportunity to experience what Sharon Wegscheider-Cruse calls "the phenomenal ability of the human body, psyche, and soul to reframe, reexamine, refeel, re-create, and reheal." I wanted to include newcomers as well as old-timers; Overeaters Anonymous fellowship members as well as people striving to overcome eating disorders with other kinds of support; those of you floating on the pink cloud of first freedom from compulsive eating or bulimia as well as those of you who have yet to experience it; those of you who manage to hang on to that freedom but live in fear of losing it; and even you who knew that freedom before you fell off the wagon.

Who Am I?

I am a helping professional with a master's degree in social work and considerable experience treating individuals and families with a wide array of problems, including eating disorders. I have collaborated on or coauthored more than a dozen self-help books. And I am also a recovering compulsive eater who has been physically abstinent since 1987, maintained a sixty-pound weight loss since 1988, and experienced most of the trials and tribulations I describe in this book. Although this isn't a book about my recovery, pieces of my personal story do appear in it—and I must admit, I agonized over including them.

As I see it, if helping professionals had to be perfect and problem-free, there would be none. Psychologists, psychiatrists, social workers, and such are human, fallible, and, in at least the same ratio found in the general population, suffering from an eating disorder or in recovery from one. However, while they are in their helping role, they generally keep their private lives and troubles to themselves. Before I began to write this book, I considered doing that too. I knew that I could easily and legitimately present myself as an expert and never discuss my own eating disorder or the victories and defeats I've experienced in recovery. But I also believed that what I had *done* before and after I took my first step toward recovery could be as valuable to other people as what I knew about eating disorders, recovery, and effectively dealing with daily living. In the end, that belief won out, and I decided to wear both hats, to include both my professional know-how and my personal experiences in this book.

When I'm wearing my recovering overeater hat and sharing my personal experiences, I'm *not* setting myself up as a sterling example of recovery. I'm just another compulsive eater, no better or worse than any other. On the way down and the way back up, I have felt and thought and done things that other people recovering from eating disorders will be able to relate to. My hope is that by baring a bit of my soul, I'll help you catch a glimpse of your own.

When I talk *about* eating disorders and recovery and suggest techniques for you to try, I'll be speaking from an "expert's" stance—objectively and authoritatively. Wearing my helping professional hat, I'll explore whys and wherefores, what works and what doesn't. I'll cover ideas and strategies that I have benefited from in my own life as well as those that seem to work wonders for other compulsive eaters and bulimics. My hope is that you will accept the validity of that objective advice, try it yourself, and keep using the techniques that work for you.

Why Did I Write This Book?

I have my friend Amy to thank for that. At age thirty-four, Amy emerged from a decade of bingeing and purging and a lifetime of compulsive eating, obsessive dieting, self-loathing, fear, and resentment. Gone were the days of weighing two hundred pounds and contemplating suicide. She had a new body, a new way of eating and relating to food, a new attitude toward life in general.

Amy had learned everything she could about bulimia. With the help of a support group, books, workshops, and some individual therapy, she had come to understand how and why the eating disorder had nearly destroyed her life. Amy had confronted demons from her past and worked hard to repair relationships with the relatives and friends who had suffered because of her bulimia. And now she could proudly declare, "I'm truly a new person with a wonderful new life."

There was just one problem, Amy noted in exasperation: "I don't know how to live it!"

It wasn't that Amy didn't know how to live. She had been on her own since she'd left her parents' home at seventeen. She had put herself through college and graduate school, had a relatively successful career, and had married. "It's pressure situations and things that come up unexpectedly," Amy explained, "people who disappoint me or lie to me, all the little bumps in the road that used to send me straight to the nearest convenience store or fast-food restaurant. Those are the things that still baffle me. I know how to go on eating binges because of them and how to work my recovery program so that I don't binge anymore, but I *don't know how to really deal with them right then and there*."

This didn't come as a complete surprise to Amy. After all, if she had known how to handle stress and problems effectively, she probably would never have developed an eating disorder. She certainly hadn't learned many coping skills while she holed up with her "best friend"—food—or devoted herself to whatever new diet she'd convinced herself would turn her life around. "And bingeing and purging didn't teach me anything about living," Amy said, cringing at the secrecy, dishonesty, isolation, and progressive "nonliving" that her bulimia had caused.

In recovery, Amy had replaced her self-destructive habits with support group meetings, phone calls to fellow eating disorder sufferers, food planning, meditation, and other measures. This was a vast improvement over her past behavior, and Amy definitely wanted her recovery program in her life. "But it's started to *be* my life," she groaned. "I don't want to define myself *solely* as a recovering bulimic or rely so heavily on clean abstinence and how many meetings I attend or phone calls I make to feel good about myself." That would leave her only slightly better off than she had been when her emotional state and sense of self-worth depended on other people's approval, mood-altering foods, constant activity, or the numbers on her bathroom scale.

"It's time for me to stop walking into the future backward," she said. "I want to turn around, face new challenges, and pursue the dreams I left behind when I started living for my next 'food fix.' " Unfortunately, it was at about that time that she had stopped growing psychologically. "I may look like an adult," Amy continued, "but when it comes to certain things—like getting to know new people or standing up for myself at work or being honest about my feelings with my husband—I have the emotional maturity of an eight-year-old."

That was hardly a sturdy foundation for her wonderful new life, Amy realized, and when she thought about all the catching up she had to do, she felt disheartened. In fact, when it dawned on her that she "knew how to be sick and how not to get sick again, but next to nothing about how to live well," she became downright depressed. "Now I have more work to do," she moaned, "and more chances to mess things up for myself." That prospect terrified her. "What I need," she exclaimed, "is a crash course in living."

If you are in the process of learning about, facing up to, or recovering from an eating disorder and don't share Amy's sentiments yet, I can virtually guarantee that one day you will.

Once we choose recovery over compulsive eating or bulimia, our future holds countless opportunities to succeed, but also to fail; to be delighted, but also to be disappointed; to have new adventures, closer relationships, and spiritual awakenings, but also to find ourselves in situations that had previously frustrated, defeated, or demoralized us. There are no guarantees, no foolproof methods, to predict outcomes accurately or control them. At some point, we all recognize this and realize that we can't "eat our way through" those situations the way we used to *or* count on the rituals and routines of recovery programs *alone* to pull us through.

Like Amy, we'll stand at a crossroads, wanting our life to be full of peace, prosperity, friendships, joy, intimacy, physical health, and more, but wondering, *How do I get that? What am I supposed to do next? And what can I do that will work better than the things I've done in the past?*

From my own experiences and those of hundreds of recovering compulsive eaters and bulimics, I have come to believe that the ability to answer those questions is the key to lasting recovery. When Amy mentioned that she'd never seen a book that addressed them, I decided to write one.

What to Expect from This Book

This book's basic premise is that *it's never too late to learn the things that no one has taught us.* Those things include reasonable, moderate eating habits, self-acceptance, and new ways of relating to people, as well as the life skills and attitudes that a client of mine refers to as "the really nitty-gritty, down-and-dirty, do-it-now stuff that I need in the middle of a crisis or when I'm under a lot of stress."

This book reflects my conviction that embarking on any program of recovery gives us an opportunity to start over and a chance to live well after so many years of being sick. But we can't benefit from that opportunity unless we *reeducate* ourselves. In order to let go of self-destructive habits, resist the temptation to return to them, and move on to new heights of wellness, we need the physical abstinence, psychological insights, and spirituality traditionally associated with recovery programs. We also need a repertoire of concrete, immediately applicable techniques for effectively dealing with unsettling emotions, stressful events, and unpleasant interactions with other people. That is what this book offers you.

I think of it as a survival kit. It is intended to help you handle whatever life throws at you—not perfectly, of course, but well enough so that you don't harm yourself or anyone else or return to self-destructive habits or start *overworking* your recovery program.

As they have for me and other eating disorder sufferers, the ideas presented here will help you move ahead without constantly looking over your shoulder to see if your eating disorder is gaining on you. You will be able to take personal and professional risks, get involved in new relationships, and try activities that you used to think of as off-limits—without worrying that experiencing failure will destroy you or jeopardize your recovery.

On the pages that follow, you'll have plenty of opportunities to gain new insights about yourself, obtain new information about compulsive eating and bulimia, and be inspired by the real-life experiences of fellow sufferers in recovery.

You'll also read about the nature of eating disorders and their probable causes. However, I'll leave that topic rather quickly in order to cover one that hasn't been written about as extensively: the most useful methods for solving recovery problems.

The emphasis throughout this book is on moving from knowing to *doing*, from feeling feelings to *effectively coping* with them, and from living in fear of relapse to *truly embracing the gifts of recovery and leading healthy and happy lives from this day forward.*

This book is not a guide to working the Twelve Steps of Overeaters Anonymous or a substitute for professional treatment, but rather a compatible companion piece for either or both. It is based on a thorough review of existing eating disorder and recovery literature, conversations with various experts in those fields, my personal and professional experiences, and the experiences of hundreds of other compulsive eaters and bulimics whom I have counseled or spoken to after workshops or OA meetings.

What's the Best Way to Use This Book?

Any way that suits *you*. While I'd like you to read this book from beginning to end, what I'd like more is for you to get all you can from this book. If you prefer, go straight to the Self-Help Index at the back of the book. Look up anger or fear or stress management, and try out the techniques described there. Or begin at the beginning and, for the first or fiftieth time, get a clear picture of where an eating disorder can take you and what you learn (or don't learn) along the way.

If your greatest struggle at the moment is with food, check out the chapter on abstinence first, but don't expect to find a quick-weight-loss diet plan there. If you're feeling discouraged and not at all sure that recovery will be worth the work, turn directly to the chapter on wellness. It shows you how to create a personal vision of a positive future and allow it to serve as the proverbial light at the end of the tunnel. And if things in your life seem to be at a standstill even though you are working your recovery program with all your might, turn to the "Hooked on Recovery" chapter. It won't be comfortable reading, but you may find ideas to break up the logjam and get you moving again.

In addition, I highly recommend that you obtain a notebook and complete as many of the writing exercises as you can. There are no right answers, and no one will grade your grammar or punctuation. Just grab a pen and let yourself go. The insights and ideas that flow onto the written page will surprise, delight, and quite often free you from some burden or resentment you've been carrying around for years.

Finally, because you and I and anyone else who is struggling to overcome an eating disorder are at different points in the recovery process and have unique needs and personalities, not everything in this book will feel appropriate. It doesn't have to. But try not to let ideas, exercises, or sections of this book that rub you the wrong way or seem irrelevant prevent you from taking advantage of other ideas, exercises, and so on.

Instead, take what you need and leave the rest. Actually test out the methods you find in this book. Think of yourself as a scientist conducting an experiment. Nothing here will blow up the lab, and you can always call things off if they don't work out.

Just keep in mind that new attitudes and behaviors always feel strange and uncomfortable at first. Be patient. Practice. Pray, if you're so inclined. Then decide what you'll keep to use in your new life and what you'll set aside, at least for now. If, in a month or a year, you find that you could use something you left behind, you can always come back for it.

PART I

THE NATURE OF THE BEAST

CHAPTER ONE

Thin is Not Well

The speaker was slender, well dressed, and in her mid-forties. Her name was Ruth, and from where I sat, slouched down in my chair with my arms defensively folded across my then massive torso, she seemed to personify recovery: perfect, permanent recovery . . . complete, "I'll-never-again-have-to-worry-about-being-fat-or-unhappy" recovery. I came to that conclusion after one quick, envious glance at her perfect size-eight figure. "She probably has a perfect career, husband, home, and kids to go with it," the green-eyed monster within me whispered. And almost as if she'd heard it too, Ruth set the record straight.

"Don't let appearances deceive you," she said—and then used a phrase that would stick with me for years to come. "*Thin isn't well.* My weight and how I look on the outside don't change how I think and feel on the inside—and *that's* what does me in. That's what I can't deal with. I *know* how to get thin. Just go on a diet! Dozens of times I've dieted until I was thin—or close to it. But I didn't stay that way. I didn't even feel comfortable that way." Ruth continued, "It was only a matter of time until I went back to my old ways—because I had sick attitudes and sick feelings and sick habits that sent me running to the refrigerator at the first sign of trouble. It could be a fender bender or the insulting remark one of my co-workers made, worrying about failing a test, or getting an invitation to my high school reunion—you name it, I would eat over it. That's what my eating disorder made me do."

Like Ruth and most of the other people who heard her speak that day, I too had "eaten" over anything and everything. I'd eaten *when I should have* asserted myself, *after* I had committed myself to do something I didn't want to do, *rather than* finding time for myself, and *before* attempting things I feared would be too much for me. If asked, I could have told you that food wouldn't cure every ill, answer every question, or solve all my problems, but I acted as if it could. And I'd been acting that way for a long, long time.

The Making of a Compulsive Eater

My first memory of compulsive eating dates back to the third grade, when our family doctor discovered that I had a congenital hip defect. Along with prescribing a number of frightening treatments involving electrical currents that made my legs twitch and tingle, he confined me to bed for several months. I was bored, lonely, and terrified, sure that I actually had a permanently crippling condition or, worse yet, a terminal illness. When I voiced that fear, my parents' response did not console me. "Don't be silly," they said. But that only told me it was silly to talk about dying—not that I wasn't.

The housekeeper with whom I was left while both of my parents worked was no more comforting. By early afternoon, when she hid out in her room with a peanut butter jar full of vodka and her TV tuned in to the soap operas, she wasn't even accessible. And that was when I ate. At first I sneaked out of bed and into the kitchen merely to break the monotony and prove that I was still able-bodied enough to make it down a flight of stairs. I gobbled up whatever I could get my hands on and then returned to my room, feeling as if I'd been on a great and dangerous mission. I went on dozens of those missions after that, sometimes venturing to other parts of the house, but always making at least one "pit stop" in the kitchen.

I started bringing food back to my bedroom with me, hiding whole bags of cookies or packages of lunch meat under my blankets and munching on them throughout the day. I wasn't so bored anymore or so scared. I hardly ever thought about being lonely or worried about being on my deathbed. If I started to, I pushed those thoughts away. Then I reached for my secret cache of food or went on a secret mission to replenish it.

My mother must have noticed that food was missing, but she never said a word. Nor did anyone mention how big I'd become—until I returned to school. As a brainy bookworm new to the school before I left it, I'd been teased some and kept on the social periphery. But that was red-carpet treatment in comparison to the cruelty I encountered when I got back. As an eight-year-old butterball with a limp and hideous oxblood-red corrective shoes, I was a complete outcast, the object of ridicule, wisecracks, and whispers.

Telling myself that I didn't care and didn't need those kids as friends anyway, I retreated. I took refuge in books, my imagination, and my secret forays into the kitchen. There I found sweet things to kill the sour taste of rejection and ate lots of them to fill up the empty space where friendship and acceptance might have been.

As the years passed, I put food to many other uses, none of them even remotely related to physical hunger. When something I did went well, I rewarded myself with food. When it didn't, food was my consolation prize. I ate when I was lonely, tired, anxious, elated, or bored. I went on "I'll show you" binges after being criticized or negated. Like a drunk or drug addict blotting out reality with booze or heroin, I ate myself into oblivion, dulling my senses and stuffing feelings of sadness or fear.

Of course, back then I wasn't consciously aware of what I was doing. As a ten-year-old, I didn't think, "I got picked last for basketball again. I guess I'll go wolf down a package of Yodels." And twenty years later, I never told myself, "Gee, Susan, you're dateless, the heater's on the fritz, and your last client made vague references to suicide. Why don't you go to a convenience store, buy twenty dollars' worth of junk food and eat it all by midnight?"

I rarely noticed unsettling emotions or realized that something was upsetting me. Before that information reached me, a self-preservation switch in my brain was flipped, converting dangerous ideas and emotions into hunger pangs or food cravings. Instead of feeling depressed or frustrated, I felt like eating ice cream. And after I polished off an entire quart of it, I felt like having something salty. Sometimes I would keep that up until I felt drugged and fell asleep. Invariably I would look back on what I'd done with complete self-disgust, and after browbeating myself unmercifully, I'd swear that I'd never, under any circumstances, allow my eating to rage out of control again. I always broke that vow.

Although many years would pass before I recognized why I was doing all that eating, I was acutely aware of its inevitable outcome—unwanted pounds, ten, thirty, and eventually more than one hundred of them. They became my enemy, the scapegoat on which I blamed *all* of my misery. I can still remember myself at thirteen, lying in bed at night begging God to make me thin. "Show me a diet that works and help me stick to it," I prayed, "and you'll never hear me complain about anything again." I sincerely believed that once I lost weight, I would have nothing to complain about. In my mind, thin was not only well, it was nirvana.

Shedding those excess pounds wouldn't just silence my father's sneering admonitions to exercise a little willpower or merely get my mother to stop warning me that she'd soon have to purchase my dresses from Omar the Tentmaker. It wouldn't just save me from being mortified when the school nurse yelled out my weight on "weigh day" or simply spare me from my classmates' cruel comments. No, shrinking my body down to a smaller size would do much more than that. It would, I thought, improve every imaginable aspect of my life.

Losing weight would make anything that was "bad"—including things completely unrelated to my weight—"all better." People would automatically like me. No one would ever reject me. My problems would melt away along with my fat, and my insecurities would vanish. I would be happy all the time.

Growing Older, But Not Wiser

For the next two decades, I clung to the magical belief that being fat was my only real problem and that being thin was the key to living happily ever after. Since I knew of only one way to get thin—dieting strenuously—that's what I did. Repeatedly. I became an avid participant in one of America's national pastimes—the pursuit of slimness—and in many ways I excelled at it. In fact, if trophies were given for pounds lost, I'd have closets full of them.

All told, I must have dropped a thousand pounds—at Weight Watchers, Diet Center, and Nutri/System; with the "help" of a half-dozen different amphetamine-prescribing diet doctors; and on most of the quick-weight-loss plans that appear on bookstore shelves or the pages of popular magazines. I was a great dieter. Unfortunately, I was a much better compulsive eater.

I loved the sense of power and self-control I felt at the beginning of each new diet, the rush of pride and optimism that accompanied each pound or inch lost, and the relief and bravado when I stayed on a diet long enough to reach my goal weight. I was always sure that this time I had the problem licked for good, the war on fat won forever. I was always wrong.

Like 90 percent of all weight losers, I gained back every pound and then some—because *thin isn't well. Because not once during all my years of rigorous dieting did I change much more than the numbers on my bathroom scale.* Sure, I'd receive lots of compliments, feel more self-confident, and be a bit more outgoing. Sometimes I managed to keep the weight off for as long as a year. But sooner or later, some problem for which there was no easy solution would arise, and before I knew it, I'd be doing what I'd always done before—reaching for the food.

My guilt, frustration, and feelings of personal failure over breaking my diet would compound the problem and provide the fuel for an amazingly rapid return to my old habit of eating until I was oblivious. I'd gain weight, go on another diet, lose weight again, trip over reality again, eat again, diet again, ad infinitum. In the meantime, my life was going on without me. Dreams I told myself I'd fulfill when I was thin slipped further from my grasp. Opportunities passed me by, and the daily problems I ignored while focusing on my weight worsened.

Didn't I see what I was doing? you may wonder. Why didn't I stop it? I used to wonder about that myself. After all, I wasn't stupid. I was a therapist, for Pete's sake, a trained professional who *should* have known better, who *should* have used my helping skills to help myself. But the truth is, I couldn't. For one thing, my habits of anesthetizing myself with food and trying to fix my life with diets were deeply ingrained and automatic. For another, I was in the grips of something much more powerful than I imagined—a disorder that doesn't pick its victims on the basis of their profession, race, religion, economic status, or IQ scores. What's more, an eating disorder comes with a satchelful of rationalizations and flat-out delusions that prevent even the most astute observers from seeing the problem in themselves.

Our Inner Propaganda Machine

Every eating disorder includes a built-in mechanism for perpetuating itself—a subconscious, selective blindness called denial. We may deny that we have a problem or deny that it's causing anyone harm. We may tell ourselves and anyone who has the audacity to question us that we have the situation under control, that we can stop overeating or bingeing and purging at any time. The right time just hasn't arrived yet. Other people who do some of the same things we do might flunk out of school or lose jobs or destroy their marriages, but such things would never happen to us, we insist. And if they do or if we become physically ill or get caught stealing from the local convenience store, we say, "This isn't so bad," or "Things could be worse," or "It's bad all right, but it has nothing to do with my eating habits or weight-control methods."

These are untruths, every one of them. But we are not really lying. We believe our own words. We are presenting reality as we see it. It's just that denial distorts reality to protect us from the things we are afraid of or unprepared to face. This distortion is a psychological defense mechanism that buffers us from thoughts, feelings, or events that we are *temporarily* unable to address or accept.

By concealing or camouflaging facts or minimizing their impact, defense mechanisms get us through crises and painful adjustment periods as safely and "normally" as possible. We go on with our lives as if nothing happened, until we are ready to face what has happened, deal with it, and move on. Unfortunately, those of us with eating disorders rarely reach that point on our own. For reasons I'll discuss in later chapters, we have such a powerful need to continue doing what we've been doing that we can't see just how dangerous and destructive our behavior has become. But sooner or later we must.

No one can overcome an eating disorder while the shield of denial is in place. Indeed, facing the cold, hard facts about our compulsive eating, obsessive dieting, or bulimia is the first thing we must do if we want to leave the behavior behind us. Recovery begins when we recognize and acknowledge just what we're up against and how formidable a foe it can be.

What We're Up Against

Eating for reasons other than physical hunger is commonplace in our culture. Food and feelings are inextricably linked almost from birth. Feeding time brings infants not only the nourishment they need to survive but also the comforting presence of the feeder and evidence that their basic needs will be met. As they get older, children receive lollipops for being brave in the pediatrician's office, ice cream cones for being good, and cookies to put smiles back on their faces after they skin their knees. They see bread broken as a symbol of friendship or respect, food used to welcome neighbors or console grieving relatives, and sweets offered as bribes, apologies, and tokens of affection.

The Pillsbury Doughboy doesn't have to tell children that "nothin' says lovin' like something from the oven." By the time they reach adulthood, most men and women have countless memories—both conscious and unconscious—linking food to the fulfillment of any imaginable need. Consequently, when they feel needy today, they may reach for the comfort foods of their childhoods or plow their way through a king-size bag of nacho chips before they realize what they're doing. Since they've also received countless parental, cultural, and media messages about the virtues of slimness and the horrors of being overweight, they may feel bad in the aftermath of eating sprees and vow to restrict their food intake the next day. They may even go on extreme diets now and then, losing five or ten pounds in a matter of days and then gaining most of them back when they return to normal eating. However, they are not likely to do any of those things to the extent that those of us with eating disorders do.

For us, the urge to use food, dieting, or bingeing and purging to satisfy psychological needs or bring about mood changes is a *compulsion*—a powerful, usually irresistible impulse to engage in certain behaviors again and again. Our preoccupation with weight, body size, eating, or not eating is an *obsession*—a persistent, repetitive idea that intrudes upon our consciousness, overrides other thought processes, and haunts us until we somehow relieve it, usually through a compulsive act. We experience what the American Psychiatric Association's *Diagnostic and Statistical Manual of Mental Disorders, Third Edition—Revised* (DSM-III-R) calls a "gross disturbance in eating behavior" and a distorted way of thinking that is much more than

- a "weight" problem
- a matter of loving food too much or having too little willpower
- something a diet can fix or having a slim, trim figure will change for long

Compulsive Eating

The vicious circle of "doing and undoing" that I was trapped in for so many years is the hallmark of any eating disorder. Most compulsive eaters can recount eating and dieting histories remarkably similar to my own, in that they

- consciously or unconsciously use food (or eating) to enhance positive moods or alter negative ones, cope with stress, manage anxiety, squelch anger, or take their minds off their problems
- eat more than their bodies require, more than their latest diet demands, or large quantities of certain foods (sweets, chips, white bread, cheese) that they find irresistible—and afterward feel guilty, depressed, disgusted with themselves, or out of control

- expend a great deal of time, attention, and emotional energy worrying about their weight, body size, and what, when, where, or how much they could, should, or did eat
- repeatedly try to control their weight and out-of-control eating through diets, fasts, excessive exercise, even surgery—all to no avail

Bulimia

Bulimics *do* (binge-eat) and *undo* (purge) one right after another—in some instances, several times a day. In addition to having many of the same traits as compulsive eaters, they rapidly consume in a distinct time period large quantities of generally high-calorie, sweet, soft, easily swallowed foods or moderate amounts of foods they've unsuccessfully forbidden themselves to eat. Their binges may be planned in advance or spontaneously triggered by the first "forbidden" bite. Binges are usually kept secret but may be shared with "binge buddies" and can be quite costly. Despite personal food preferences, bulimics intent upon bingeing will consume anything they can find or afford. Bulimia sufferers typically

- block out all emotions during the binge, but the instant it ends feel intense shame, panic, self-loathing, and terror at the prospect of gaining weight
- immediately attempt to silence self-recriminations, relieve physical fullness and emotional pressure, and get rid of food and calories by purging—usually through self-induced vomiting, but sometimes with laxatives, diuretics, hours of aerobic exercise, or fasting; by "undoing" their binges in this manner, bulimics often can keep their weight within normal range, give or take ten pounds
- suffer a number of medical complications, such as fatigue, a sore throat, an ulcerated esophagus, tooth decay, potassium depletion, and more
- are driven to continue their bingeing and purging even though they are aware that it isn't normal, almost always feel horribly ashamed of it, and start most days vowing never to do it again

It is not unusual for bulimics to spend nearly every waking hour fighting the urge to eat. Nor is it uncommon for them to fear that one day they'll start eating and be unable to stop voluntarily.

Anorexia

For anorexics, the mere thought of what they could *do*—eat "too much" and get fat—triggers their *undoing* behavior: self-starvation. Although a detailed discussion of the attitudes, behaviors, and treatment needs of anorexics is beyond the scope of this book, anorexics do bear certain resemblances to compulsive eaters on diets and to bulimics (which anorexics may become after treatment returns them to their normal weight). They lose 15 percent to 25 percent of their body weight, refuse to maintain normal or even near-normal body weight, and gain a heady sense of power, control, self-sufficiency, and "specialness" by purposely eating as little as possible or, if possible, nothing at all.

What frequently starts out as "typical" dieting becomes more and more extreme. In general, anorexics

- are terrified of becoming obese, believe they are fat despite all evidence to the contrary, and tend to exercise excessively and obsessively

- may talk incessantly about food, diets, and exercise or prepare elaborate meals for others; they are actually hungry most of the time, but avoid calories at all costs—including dizziness, numb hands and feet, dehydration, low blood pressure, heart irregularities, kidney problems, potassium depletion, nutritional imbalances, loss of menstrual periods, and worse

- lie about and ingeniously conceal their weight loss and lack of eating; use guilt, blame, anger, and manipulation to fend off anyone who expresses concern about their condition; and can rarely be convinced that they have a problem without intensive professional help, including, for some, forced hospitalization to prevent starvation

- offer visible proof that thin is not well. Untreated anorexia can be fatal and is for 5 percent to 18 percent of those who suffer from it

If any of the foregoing patterns seemed familiar to you, the thoughts, feelings, and behaviors in the following self-test may too.

❦

MORE EATING DISORDER SYMPTOMS—A SELF-TEST

Below each item, check the answer that comes closest to describing you. If you have been in recovery for a while and some items no longer apply, base your answers on what you used to be like (and then pat yourself on the back for the progress you've made).

Do you worry a great deal about your weight or body size, perhaps weighing yourself several times a day or repeatedly comparing yourself to others and wishing you could look like them?

_____ almost always _____ often _____ sometimes
_____ occasionally _____ almost never

Do you feel as if your life is dominated by conflicts about eating (lots of shoulds and shouldn'ts where food is concerned)?

_____ almost always _____ often _____ sometimes
_____ occasionally _____ almost never

Do you suffer from bouts of depression or panic?

_____ almost always _____ often _____ sometimes
_____ occasionally _____ almost never

Do you have problems with excessive drinking; drug, laxative, or diuretic use; gambling; or spending?

_____ almost always _____ often _____ sometimes
_____ occasionally _____ almost never

Are you still overeating or yo-yo dieting despite one or more of the following medical complications: hypertension, arteriosclerosis, diabetes, gallbladder disease, or impaired breathing?

_____ almost always   _____ often   _____ sometimes

_____ occasionally   _____ almost never

Do you isolate yourself, staying at home or keeping an emotional distance from people because they might reject you, criticize you, try to change your eating habits, or delay or interfere with what you'd rather be doing (that is, eating or bingeing and purging)?

_____ almost always   _____ often   _____ sometimes

_____ occasionally   _____ almost never

Will you restructure your day to make it easier for you to eat, not eat, binge and purge, or exercise for extended periods of time?

_____ almost always   _____ often   _____ sometimes

_____ occasionally   _____ almost never

Are you secretive (for example, eating like a bird in front of others and then pigging out when you're alone, hiding food, or going to great lengths to conceal the fact that you've recently vomited)?

_____ almost always   _____ often   _____ sometimes

_____ occasionally   _____ almost never

Do you resent people who comment on your weight or eating habits, and do you become defensive if anyone tries to suggest that you do something about them?

_____ almost always   _____ often   _____ sometimes

_____ occasionally   _____ almost never

Despite all evidence to the contrary—including the fact that you've tried and failed many times—do you insist that you can get your eating, dieting excesses, or bingeing and purging under control whenever you make up your mind to?

_____ almost always   _____ often   _____ sometimes
_____ occasionally   _____ almost never

❧

Right now, those of you who answered the majority of the preceding questions with "occasionally" or "almost never" may be thinking, *I'm not that messed up. Maybe my therapist (or doctor or recovering friend) was wrong and I don't have an eating disorder after all.* Although that may be the case, if something moved you to pick up this book, it probably isn't. So please think again.

Every eating disorder sufferer does not necessarily have every symptom or have symptoms in only their most severe form. What's more, looking at what we *are not* in order to argue that what we *are* isn't so bad is one of the tricks denial leads us to play on ourselves. Once we've minimized our problem, there's no need to feel as rotten about it or to fix it. Finally, if we're willing to wait, there's a good chance that the symptoms we don't have today will appear six months, a year, or five years from now, and the ones we do have will have intensified. Unacknowledged and untreated eating disorders take all of us in only one direction—further and further downhill.

The Downhill Journey

Marjorie, thirty-two and recovering from bulimia, knows that journey all too well. She describes herself as "a lifelong emotional eater who got away with it until I left home for the first time to attend college—and found a whole lot more to eat over." There was the ache of missing her parents and friends, the shock of being "nothing but a number" on a huge campus after being a star in her small hometown, the noise and lack of privacy in her dormitory, and, as she puts it, "just an overwhelming sense that I didn't fit in." By spring break, she had added twenty-five pounds to her five-foot-two-inch frame.

"It didn't come off as easily as those five pounds I'd been gaining in the winter and losing in time for summer since I turned fourteen," Marjorie recalls. She kept cutting back on her food consumption and increasing her activity until she was living on "rabbit food" and exercising several hours daily. Marjorie started her sophomore year thirty pounds lighter than she'd been three months earlier. Once back at school, however, her resolve crumbled. She began to gain weight.

But then she got to know Becky, a sorority sister who "could eat anything without getting fat," and learned her secret—self-induced vomiting. "At first, I didn't think I could do it," Marjorie remembers. "Then I couldn't believe I *was* doing it. But it definitely worked. I still watched what I ate, but instead of making myself miserable if I ate too much, I just got rid of the extra calories by making myself puke."

Marjorie purged no more than once or twice a week back then and never at home. "In the summer, I exercised a lot and fasted on the day after I ate too much, but I didn't purge," she explains. However, the solitary bingeing and purging became a weekly ritual once Marjorie moved to New York City and took what she called a "lowly" copyediting position at a major magazine.

"I would start planning the binge on Wednesday," she recalls, "putting away money for it, making food lists, checking restaurants for private bathrooms, sometimes even drawing up a map of where I'd go for what." By Friday night it was difficult for her to think of anything else. And when Sunday rolled around, she was more than ready to "eat my way across Manhattan, running up credit card bills and throwing up every morsel I swallowed. It was an unbelievable release, all of it. And yes, if I had really thought about it, I would have been repulsed by what I was doing. But I wasn't. The way I looked at it, my Sunday eat-a-thons were the only pleasurable part of my entire miserable existence."

When Marjorie's existence changed, so did her behavior. The ritualistic weekly binges stopped completely one month after she met Don, her husband-to-be. However, at least once a week, right up until she became pregnant with her first child, she continued to eat more than she thought she should and undo the damage by vomiting. "During my pregnancy," Marjorie says, "I felt so responsible for my unborn child that I ate sensibly, exercised moderately, really took care of both of us." Everyone at the magazine, where she had worked her way up to senior editor, marveled at how slim she was just weeks before the delivery. For months afterward, the joys and demands of new motherhood provided natural weight control. "I didn't even think about bingeing or purging. I was happier than I'd ever been in my life."

Unfortunately, her euphoria evaporated when, less than a year after she returned to her job, she discovered she was pregnant again. She says, "I was doing okay with a career and one child. But two? So soon? I couldn't deal with it." Marjorie wanted to abort the pregnancy, but her husband wouldn't hear of it. Their heated argument on the subject ended with him walking out of the house and Marjorie going on an eating binge. "I ate anything that was handy," she confesses, "and I didn't stop until I thought I'd explode. Then I vomited and started over again." After she had gone through this cycle three times, she calmly cleaned up the kitchen and went to bed.

For the next month, Marjorie binged and purged in this frenzied manner at least once and sometimes two or three times daily. She might have kept it up for longer if she hadn't started worrying about the harm she might be causing her unborn child and once again realized that she was responsible for another life. This time around, however, that sense of responsibility only prevented her from purging. She ate "like there was no tomorrow" and gained close to eighty pounds during her pregnancy.

Having already gone from annual weight gains and losses during adolescence to purging for weight control to various forms of bingeing and purging—each more severe than the one before— and compulsive eating, Marjorie would continue to alternate periods of relative well-being with episodes of food abuse for another four years. "Only the good times kept getting shorter," she notes, "and the bad times kept getting worse."

Can't Win for Losing

For those of us with eating disorders, the bad times always got worse. When the pizza, pretzels, and one-pound bag of Halloween candy were all gone . . . or there was nothing left in our stomachs to purge . . . or we awakened groggy and confused, walked into the living room, and saw the foil and cardboard containers of the previous night's eating marathon . . . that's when the self-loathing set in. Out came the self-condemning, self-recriminating, self-abusive thoughts. They made us feel sicker and sicker inside, so sick that we soon needed something to make us feel better. And what we instinctively reached for to cure our emotional hangover was the "hair of the dog that bit us"—more food or compulsive behavior.

We had established a pattern of soothing ourselves with a mood-altering substance or activity, then yelling at ourselves for doing so, and, as a result, creating a need for more soothing, which we responded to with more behavior that we would wind up yelling at ourselves for doing.

It was a classic lose-lose situation, because the harder we tried to control our behavior with guilt, shame, and self-criticism that we felt compelled to relieve by overeating or bingeing and purging, *the more uncontrollable that behavior became*. As I explain in the next chapter, this loss of control is found in any addiction, which I, as well as numerous experts on compulsive eating and bulimia, believe an eating disorder is.

CHAPTER TWO

Losing Control:
Eating Disorders as Addictions

Four years after the birth of her second child, Marjorie's promising career as a magazine editor was long gone. She had abandoned it when little Donnie turned out to be a sickly child in need of more attention than any baby-sitter was willing to give him. Marjorie felt responsible for his ill health and his cranky temperament too. She sometimes thought he was making her pay for not wanting him initially, or for bingeing and purging during the first trimester of her pregnancy, or for gaining so much weight in the final two trimesters that she nearly killed them both.

Marjorie had lost that weight a half-dozen times since then but could never seem to keep it off without purging. This habit so disgusted her husband, Don, that each time he caught her at it—and he always managed to—a huge argument followed and did not end until Marjorie swore that she would never make herself vomit again. But she always did. "God knows I tried," Marjorie says, "*but I just couldn't stop.*"

Neither could Carl, a twenty-eight-year-old stockbroker and compulsive eater. "Once upon a time," he recalls. "I could stick to a diet. I could have one small snack a couple of hours after dinner and then go to bed. A bag of cookies could last for a week." Not anymore. "Now I can't stop eating anything until it's all gone," he says. "I spend entire evenings either doing nothing but eating or fighting losing battles to resist the urge to eat. The other night, I actually took a sleeping pill and went to bed at eight o'clock just so I'd stop picking at something I was supposed to be bringing to an office party the next day."

Carl tossed and turned and finally stumbled out of bed supposedly to use the bathroom. "I swore I wouldn't even go into the kitchen," he notes. "But the next thing I knew, that's where I was, plowing through the entire party tray, knowing I'd have to replace it and telling myself to stop. *But I just couldn't.*"

Similarly, Candace, a twenty-four-year-old bulimic from a very wealthy and, she'd add, thin family, reports, "I used to have this hard-and-fast rule, this line I swore I wouldn't cross, and that was never bingeing in front of anyone. I wanted people to think that I was a normal eater, maybe even *more* disciplined than the average person. Then when I was alone and sure no one would walk in on me, I'd make a complete pig of myself."

However, Candace wasn't able to keep her private eating habits out of the public eye indefinitely. "After a while, I just couldn't do it anymore," she says. "And I do mean *couldn't,* because I tried like crazy to get groceries back to the privacy of my apartment without digging into them. It was completely beyond me. Usually I'd duck down behind the dashboard, tear open bags, and start pushing food into my face as fast as I could. If I did get to my apartment building without doing that, I'd lose it in the elevator and start eating like a madwoman—even though I knew the security people could see me on their video monitor. I'd stare right at the camera and imagine how disgusting I must look—*but I just couldn't stop.*"

At some point, every compulsive eater or bulimic will utter those words out loud or mutter them to themselves. Like alcoholics who break every promise to quit tomorrow, or compulsive gamblers who swear they'll never place another bet but are on the phone with their bookies by the end of the day, we continue to engage in the same destructive behavior despite our determination to curtail it and our desperate efforts to control ourselves. That lack of control is just one reason why a growing number of clinicians have started to refer to their eating disorder patients as "food-addicted."

Eating Disorders as Addictions

Anything we repetitively do or put into our systems to (1) produce a euphoric state of mind, (2) avoid dealing with feelings of pain, fear, guilt, or shame, or (3) escape the problems and pressures of daily living has the potential to become an addiction. A substance or behavior becomes an addiction when we can't resist the urge to use the substance or engage in the behavior, even though it is jeopardizing our health, sanity, relationships, and other areas of our lives.

For addicts, the force driving them to drink, smoke crack, go on a shopping spree, or use their rent money to buy lottery tickets is so powerful that neither the consequences of their actions nor their own desire to stop can get them to stop. You will never meet a recovering addict who, prior to getting into recovery, hadn't thought about quitting, promised to quit, tried to quit, and failed to quit at least once—and usually many times over.

Addictions are chronic, progressive, and potentially fatal. When mood-altering substances, such as alcohol, nicotine, or heroin, are involved, the problem is at least partly physical in nature. But there is always a psychological component as well. Eventually addicts become so dependent on a substance or activity that going without it creates a multitude of unwelcome symptoms. They also lose control over their obsessions and compulsive behaviors, deny the existence or magnitude of their problem, and rarely if ever are able to solve it on their own. As you will see, compulsive eating and bulimia fit that description on all counts.

Eating Disorders Are Chronic

Once we develop eating disorders, they never go away. Our disorders may lie dormant for stretches of time. Or they may put on a new overcoat, changing from anorexia to bulimia, or from bulimia to compulsive eating, then back to bulimia again. But they always reappear in some form. That is their basic nature, and that nature doesn't change once we're in recovery.

We have a long-lasting, recurring condition. Like diabetes or alcoholism, it can be arrested and managed, but not cured. We must continue to treat it even after obvious signs of the illness, such as obesity or self-induced vomiting, disappear. No matter what size we get down to or how long we refrain from our destructive eating or dieting behaviors, our food addiction can be reactivated by consuming certain foods, being in certain situations, reaching for food when we're under pressure, eating less to drop ten pounds, or resuming any other previously problematic attitude or action.

If this is news to you, chances are that you see it as bad news. It means that your lifelong dream of waking up one morning miraculously transformed into a thin, normal eater won't be coming true. You may not be ready to give up your belief that somewhere there is a pill or diet or hypnotic suggestion that will fix you quickly and permanently. But if you set your disappointment aside for a moment, you may be able to see that accepting that you have a chronic illness and doing what it takes to keep it in remission, the way diabetics do, isn't so bad. At the very least, it frees us from the demoralizing downward spiral of trying to succeed using an approach that will continue to fail us and usually cause us to sink lower.

Eating Disorders Are Progressive

They get worse over time. But you don't need *me* to tell you that. You wouldn't be reading this book if your problem hadn't intensified over the years and eventually reached dangerous or intolerable levels.

As our eating disorders progress, we find ourselves doing things we swore we would never do . . . eating a whole pizza or gallon of ice cream at one sitting . . . eating food we've retrieved from the trash can . . . eating undefrosted cakes or breads straight from the freezer . . . stealing food or money to buy food . . . turning down invitations so we could stay home and eat . . . purging even once, or bingeing and purging more than once a month, once a week, or once a day . . . or spending an entire weekend in our apartments eating—not showering or dressing or answering the phone, just eating—all two hundred dollars' worth of groceries we bought on Friday and anything we can order in and pay for with a personal check.

The amount of money we spend on food or diet programs may increase. So will our sense of isolation as we cut back on plans and activities because we feel fat or want to conceal or maintain our "habit." Our efforts to curtail any of those behaviors will become futile. We aren't in the driver's seat. Our obsessions and compulsions are truly beyond our control.

All Eating Disorders Eventually Become Uncontrollable

Like alcoholics who periodically go on the wagon, we compulsive eaters and bulimics periodically take back the reins of control by going on diets. But over the years, these efforts are less successful and last for shorter periods of time. As our eating disorders progress, we lose control over a number of things:

- The *amount* of food we consume. We routinely eat more than we intended or promised ourselves we would.
- The *duration* of overeating episodes. We find it virtually impossible to stop eating as long as there is anything edible nearby, or we eat until we feel drugged and pass out.
- *Where and when we eat.* We may, for example, wake up in the middle of the night to eat; break our diets by 10:00 A.M.; "graze" all day or night, or both; or eat in our cars, at our desks, or secretly, such as in the bathroom stalls at work or the utility closet at home.
- *Routines and rituals* that were once predictable and comforting. We become extremely anxious or upset whenever something we planned or anticipated is delayed or interrupted, especially if that activity is in any way related to food or dieting.
- *Our tempers* or other emotions. We get upset more often, especially when someone or something comes between us and our food supply or the opportunity to purge.

◦✤◦

FROM FIRST TO LOST: AN AWARENESS EXERCISE

At age five Carl just had to have the graham crackers left over after preschool snacktime. So he stole them from the teacher's desk, hid them in his coat, and sneaked them into his mouth during recess.

"At evening meals when I was nine or ten," Marjorie says, "I would hunch over my plate trying to eat as much as I could as fast as I could before my mom and dad's bickering turned into a shouting match."

Candace went on her first diet at the age of twelve. "I thought I was humongous and disgusting," she says. "But now, when I look at old pictures, I can see that I wasn't even overweight."

Although they didn't know it at the time, these incidents were harbingers of things to come, early signs of the disturbed eating behavior and distorted thinking about food, weight, or their bodies that are hallmarks of any eating disorder. What were some of yours?

Take out the notebook that will serve as your recovery journal and write about one, several, or all of the following "firsts": The first time you can remember

- eating for reasons other than physical hunger
- craving certain foods
- worrying about your weight
- bingeing
- purging
- dieting
- feeling guilty about or trying to conceal your eating, weight, or purging
- thinking that your eating, dieting, or purging behavior was bad, strange, or sick (or being told that it was)
- vowing not to engage in certain behaviors ever again
- breaking that vow

Then, for each of the firsts you've just identified, flip through your memory bank and stop at one-, two-, or five-year intervals to mentally review (1) your eating and/or dieting behavior during those times, (2) your feelings about yourself, your weight, and your body, (3) how you judged yourself or felt other people were judging you, and (4) how your preoccupation with eating or not eating affected other areas of your life. You can also write these thoughts in your journal if you wish.

Or chart the progression of your eating disorder by selecting several of your firsts or other facets of your eating disorder and completing the following series of statements about each of them:

I started out . . . ,
then I . . . ,
then I . . . (and so on),
I thought I'd hit bottom when I . . . ,
but then I . . . (and so on).

Finally, write about losing control in any or all of the areas listed earlier in the exercise. Come up with at least one example from your own life for each area you choose.

❧

This chronicling of our decline can be depressing, humiliating, maybe even horrifying. We'll wince at the memories of things we've done and be tempted to berate ourselves for sinking so low for so long. But in a real sense, we couldn't help it. We didn't consciously choose to develop eating disorders, and by the time we got our first inkling that something was awry, we were already physically or psychologically dependent on the substances or activities that would one day bring us to our knees.

Our Problem Is Partly Physiological

Although it is not yet irrefutably proven, there appears to be a physical abnormality in the way eating disorder sufferers react to certain foods; most notably, refined sugar, processed wheat prod-

35

ucts, and junk foods high in fat or loaded with artificial flavors and preservatives. For those of us who are sensitive to one or more of those substances, the foods that contain them are like heroin to a drug addict or alcohol to an alcoholic. They bring about a sought-after mood change—calming us when we are anxious, giving us an energy boost when we're fatigued.

We tend to persistently crave these foods. And once we start eating them, we find it extremely difficult to limit the amount we consume. Some of us actually need those foods to feel normal. We are *physically dependent* on them and go through painful withdrawal when we are deprived of them for any length of time.

Eating Disorders Have a Psychological Component Too

In addition to the energized or sedated feelings certain foods produce, our moods can be altered by the acts of eating those foods, bingeing on large quantities of any food, purging, following a strict diet, or calculating and recalculating the calories we've consumed. Engaging in those behaviors and often merely thinking about them relieve tension and distract us from more unsettling matters. *Acting out*, as this behavior is called, offers excitement and escape from the mundane. It supplies us with an outlet for pent-up frustration, the illusion that we are running the show, a rush of pleasure, or merely a temporary respite from our worries.

Triggered by physical cravings or unnamed, consciously unnoticed internal uproars, acting out can involve well-planned rituals, like Marjorie's Sunday afternoon eat-a-thons. Or it can be such a quick, knee-jerk reaction that we don't see the deed until it's done. For instance, while arguing with your mother on the telephone, you could remove a carton of ice cream from the freezer and between "Yes," "No," and "That's not what I meant, Mother," plow through half of it before your consciousness catches up with you and shouts, "Look at what you're doing!"

Instead of feeling or directly dealing with inner turmoil or external conflicts, we instinctively and usually unwittingly *do* something, something that can be completely unrelated to the real source of trouble. Naturally, our action doesn't solve our problems—especially the ones stirring up anxiety from their hiding places in our subconscious minds. But it does temporarily reduce that anxiety, allow us to feel in control, or less out of control, and enable us to tune out whatever was bothering us in the first place—all of which make the activity extremely habit-forming.

We develop a psychological dependency on mood-altering activities that is just as powerful and difficult to resist as a physical one. Discontinuing those behaviors leaves us feeling anxious, crazy, or out of control.

What's really out of control is our addiction—and usually other areas of our lives as well. As we become more and more driven to fulfill the needs created by our physical or psychological dependencies, our marriages may crumble. Our children may become unruly or distant. We may suffer financially, lose jobs, or see our physical health deteriorate. Through it all, some of us will maintain at least one sacred area, such as our career, art, or ability to help others, that continues to go well, sometimes exceptionally so. But in the end, food addiction will adversely affect that area too and may even put our lives in jeopardy.

Eating Disorders Are Potentially Fatal Illnesses

If left untreated and unabated, eating disorders can lead to early graves, earliest perhaps for anorexics, who can literally starve themselves to death while still in their teens or early twenties. And if they don't, their hearts—stressed by chemical imbalances and malnutrition—may fail, a fate that sometimes befalls bulimics as well. Obese eating disorder sufferers, including those whose weight goes up and down like a yo-yo, are high-risk candidates for heart disease, respiratory problems, certain types of cancer, and deadly complications during pregnancy, childbirth, and surgery.

If the adverse effects of obesity or extreme weight-control measures don't get us, depression and suicide may. Ignored, ridiculed, even systematically discriminated against, overweight compulsive eaters and bulimics may permanently retire themselves from the uphill battle for love and acceptance. Shame and desperation over out-of-control eating or purging drive other eating disorder sufferers to similarly drastic measures. And it isn't farfetched to say that all of us with eating disorders are committing slow suicide anyway.

I know I was. My last big weight loss prior to getting into recovery nearly killed me. Nine months on an extremely low-calorie, no-fat, ostensibly supervised, for-profit program led to a hundred-pound weight loss, gallstones, and, ultimately, emergency surgery to remove my gangrenous gallbladder. A thousand miles away from home at the time, I had the dubious distinction of being the sickest patient on my hospital ward and, due to complications before and during surgery, almost a terminal one. Although the fluke of being thin at the time may have helped to save me, there was little doubt that what brought me to the brink of death in the first place was the diet that made me thin combined with all those years of abusing my body with rapid weight gains and losses.

But did this unquestionably terrifying, near-fatal experience cure me, "scare me straight," so to speak? Not quite. It would take another year and sixty pounds regained to get me to surrender, to finally say, "There's something going on here that I can't manage by myself."

Eating Disorder Sufferers Can't "Quit" on Their Own

Telling food addicts to "just say no" is an exercise in futility. We just can't do it. We may want to. We may try to. We may even manage to temporarily. But when all is said and done, our willpower alone simply won't be powerful enough to permanently stave off cravings, fight off obsessions, and resist the urge to engage in compulsive behavior.

The only way out of our addiction is through a program of recovery, one that allows us to draw upon a power greater than our own—whether a spiritual source of strength, a professional therapist, the support of other recovering individuals, or all three—and develop a new way of living and dealing with life. The good news is that once we embark upon such a path, our healing will be as progressive as our illness once was. A holistic approach to recovery, such as the one I introduce in the next chapter, not only halts the disease process but reverses it, taking us to a level of physical, emotional, and spiritual wellness that we've never known before.

CHAPTER THREE

This Way Out:
Embarking on a Program of Recovery

Marjorie's Last Binge

Midnight. Marjorie was glad to see the day end. Not that tomorrow will be any better, she thought, as she tiptoed out of her son's bedroom and heaved a weary sigh of half-relief, half-despair. Little Donnie would probably run a fever again, and she'd have to take another day off without pay to care for him. Her boss at the community newspaper would pitch a fit, but that seemed preferable to being reamed out by Donnie's nursery school teacher again. Her words and accusatory tone still rang in Marjorie's ears: "Couldn't you see how sick he was? Don't you dare bring him in here like this again. We're not a hospital, you know."

Marjorie cringed at the memory. She really was a lousy mother, she thought, and not exactly a prize of a wife. When Don called earlier, he'd said that he had a new client "almost hooked" and would be spending the night in the city so he could close the deal over breakfast. But she wondered if that was the real reason he'd decided not to come home. Maybe he just wanted to stay away from Marjorie. Could she blame him? She stared at her reflection in the full-length mirror. Although her latest diet had brought her within ten pounds of her goal weight, she saw a humongous blob, a washed-out failure. Who could possibly love her? She hated herself at that moment.

"I don't remember walking into the kitchen," Marjorie says, "or opening a cabinet or even what I ate first. I was too busy thinking that instead of being good at anything, I was mediocre at everything. I was a big fat zero."

It was at that point in her self-deprecating internal monologue that Marjorie noticed her hand methodically traveling back and forth between a bag of caramel corn and her mouth, which was filling up so rapidly that she couldn't chew fast enough to keep popcorn kernels from falling onto the floor.

Although she had sworn off bingeing and purging after a humiliating scene with Don just days earlier, Marjorie knew that was what she was about to do. "And nothing could have stopped me," she now admits.

Her kitchen was well stocked with a week's worth of groceries to feed a family of four. "I ate just about everything," Marjorie confesses. "Two quarts of ice cream, jelly on white bread, then just the bread with spoonfuls of jelly in between bites. I ate leftovers, the kids' SpaghettiOs straight from the can, frozen coffee cakes, a gallon of milk." Most of this list Marjorie compiled after the fact from the containers and wrappers she'd left behind. During the binge itself, she was, by her own admission, "an eating machine, with no thoughts, no feelings, and just one purpose—to fill myself up and empty myself out." Twice she purged without finding the relief she sought and then binged again.

"At some point, the telephone rang," Marjorie recalls, "and I vaguely remember taking it off the hook because I didn't want to be bothered by it." She was pretty vague about her last trip to the bathroom as well and was in a fog when she lay down on the living room sofa to nap before cleaning up the kitchen. Practically comatose, she didn't hear little Donnie coughing and calling out to her. She didn't respond to Katie's pleas for her to wake up and didn't stir when Don, who had rushed home after he couldn't get through to Marjorie on the telephone, entered the house. She did overhear him talking to his mother on the kitchen phone, however. He was saying that he and the kids would be staying with her for a while, maybe indefinitely.

Marjorie, her heart racing in abject terror, bolted to her feet and headed for the kitchen. Once there, she saw the destruction her binge had wrought. "And then," she says, "I wanted to die."

"At that moment," Marjorie continues, "I felt like the lowest life form, the most despicable, disgusting creature on earth. I was horrified by what I'd done—and terrified of what I'd do once Don and the kids were gone. Luckily, Don cared enough—God knows why—to have called a friend of his who was recovering from bulimia. She'd come over before, but this time I was ready to hear what she said and willing to try anything she suggested. I was so far down, I had nowhere to go but up."

Hitting Bottom and Bouncing Back

At our lowest point before beginning our recovery, we may not have eaten a week's worth of groceries and purged until we passed out. Our spouses may not have taken the kids and walked out on us. However, we undoubtedly felt the same sort of anguish and self-loathing that Marjorie did and experienced a similar sense of utter despair or panic. Our eating disorders may have cost us more or less than Marjorie's in terms of time, money, relationships, and professional success, but they took an identical toll on our self-respect. The derogatory labels we've stuck on ourselves include "undisciplined," "self-indulgent," "greedy," "weak-willed," "repulsive," and worse.

With such spirit-poisoning thoughts running through our minds and the damage we'd done to ourselves and others suddenly all too clear, we, like Marjorie, may have wanted to die and might even have seriously contemplated suicide. At the very least, we could no longer pretend that everything was fine or convince anyone—including ourselves—that we'd stop eating compulsively, dieting obsessively, or bingeing and purging on our own. We'd tried that and failed so many times before that we had no real hope left. We'd hit bottom, sunk lower, by our own standards, than we ever imagined we'd go.

At that moment, we found ourselves in a terrifying place. But it was also the place where we had nothing to lose by relinquishing our belief in quick, magical solutions and everything to gain by considering something other than the same old disheartening roller-coaster ride.

You see, hitting bottom is both a crisis and an opportunity. When we manage to break through our denial and peek through the crack in our previously impenetrable armor, we see some horrifying truths about ourselves, but also a glimmer of something out on the horizon that might save us. We can finally stop condemning ourselves and start turning our lives around if we take advantage of that insight and reach for help from Twelve Step fellowships like OA, other self-help groups, self-help books like this one, inpatient facilities, or therapists specializing in the treatment of eating disorders.

It's Not Us, It's Our Approach

For years we've been treating our eating disorders as if they were weight problems that could be easily and permanently corrected. Our treatment of choice has been a little willpower and the latest foolproof diet. And our results? Dismal. Disastrous even. Our past failures hang like albatrosses around our necks—but they are not proof that we are hopeless cases or that nothing can save us from our out-of-control eating. They point instead to some serious problems with our approach.

Relying on willpower is a bust, for instance, because willpower is no match for obsessions, compulsions, and biological factors that make us persistently crave certain foods. Trying to shame and badger ourselves into sticking to a diet only stirs up the internal uproar that we emotional eaters squelch by feeding ourselves.

Diets themselves—which have a 90 percent failure rate in the general population—are a complete washout for compulsive eaters and bulimics. Most diets don't eliminate foods that physically or psychologically trigger binges. All tend to increase our preoccupation with food, fat, and weight, fueling obsessions and compulsive behavior rather than relieving them.

Traditional psychotherapy, which some of us turn to after traditional diets fail, certainly has the potential to help us figure out why we have problems with food, body image, and the like. But such insight can only do us a limited amount of good while we are still using food as a sedative and dieting as a distraction. What we need is an approach that works on the physical and psychological aspects simultaneously, that gets us to *give up* mood-altering foods and compulsive behaviors and *pick up* coping skills, relationships, emotional support, and spiritual connectedness instead. That's what a recovery program does.

A recovery program is different from a diet or insight-oriented therapy because it acknowledges that eating disorders are chronic, progressive, addictive illnesses that can be arrested but not cured. It views us, the recovering compulsive eaters or bulimics, not as weak people who need more intestinal fortitude, but as sick people who need to get well. And it tells us, "Stop beating yourself up over a disease you did not choose to get; until now you did not know how to manage this disease."

Diets are based on the assumption that we are fat because we eat too much and need to exercise more self-control; recovery programs are based on the premise that we are *powerless to control* obsessions, compulsive behaviors, and the effect certain foods have on our bodies, minds, and spirits. Recovery programs recognize that this lack of control causes problems in many other areas of our lives and that we need to get "sober"—that is, clean, clear-thinking, free of addictive substances or behaviors—to be able to make healthy, self-enhancing choices.

We do this by becoming involved in an ongoing, multilayered process that begins when we hit bottom, admit that we have a problem with food, eating, or dieting which is adversely affecting our lives, and acknowledge that we need help to solve it. Then we

- find an expert—someone or something to guide us through the unfamiliar, often rocky terrain of early recovery—and start following his, her, or its instructions
- seek and accept support from helping professionals, fellow eating disorder sufferers, and, if we are so inclined, a spiritual source of strength
- take action to discontinue compulsive behavior and the use of addictive substances or binge foods.

As our recovery continues, we make our way out of the dark hole in which our eating disorders left us by

- unraveling the reasons for our behavior
- developing healthy relationships and a new attitude about ourselves
- learning the coping, communication, problem-solving, and self-care skills we'll need to deal with the emotions and issues we once ate over

"But That Could Take a Lifetime!"

You're right. It could, and that's another way that recovery programs differ from diets: they don't promise a quick fix or in any way encourage us to think that we can go back to our old way of eating as soon as we reach a certain weight. Recovering from something as insidious and powerful as compulsive eating, obsessive dieting, or bulimia involves making a major life-style change; surrendering old ways to make room for new attitudes and behaviors; and giving up certain foods or habits, knowing full well that ever picking them up again could reactivate our addiction.

That's scary. In fact, without even considering the amount of effort that could be required of us, words like *life-style change* and *surrender* will set off red-alert sirens. We'll rationalize, complain, and even shout, "It's not fair. Other people don't have to go to these lengths. Why do I?" The answer to that question will never change: *We have a chronic, progressive, potentially fatal illness.*

We didn't choose to develop that illness and, no, it isn't fair that we ended up with it. But railing against our disease and figuring out ways not to do what it takes to survive it aren't going to change anything. On the other hand, accepting the reality of our situation and following a treatment plan that will keep our eating disorders in check free us from the endless struggle and allow us to lead fuller lives.

If that much acceptance and stick-to-itiveness seem beyond you right now, you can, to borrow a phrase from Alcoholic Anonymous (AA), simply "suit up, show up, and act as if" you have it. Waiting to fully accept and understand your disease before taking action can be disastrous. Its progression cannot be halted nor your life reclaimed until you *stop using the substances or engaging in the behaviors that are destroying you*. The rest of this chapter discusses recommendations to help you do that:

- Turn to others for guidance, encouragement, and inspiration.
- Reach out to a power greater than yourself.
- Abstain from the foods and behaviors you can't control.
- Identify specific behaviors and substances that are addictive for you.
- Learn to recognize and deal with withdrawal symptoms.
- Tailor your food plan to fit your abstinence.
- Don't mess with success.

Turn to Others for Guidance, Encouragement, and Inspiration
No one recovers alone. In fact most of us need a whole network of knowledgeable, compassionate people to lean on and talk to, laugh with and learn from. We need mentors to share their experience with us, teachers and counselors to help us understand ourselves, fellow eating disorder sufferers to show us that we aren't the only ones who act the way we do.

It's okay to need these people. But not all people can meet your needs. Those who will be most supportive are

- people who know about eating disorders and what it takes to overcome them
- people who are available to you in person or by telephone at various hours of the day or evening and whose judgment you trust
- people with whom you will be honest
- people who are willing to tell you the truth

Some of these individuals are in your life already. They are the counselors, ministers, friends, or family members who neither coddle nor coerce you, yet are there to appreciate and motivate you as needed. You will have to go out and find other support people. Good places to look include Overeaters Anonymous meetings; eating disorder workshops, seminars or self-help groups; and clinics or centers that specialize in the treatment of food or other addictions and that offer group as well as individual counseling.

Although the people we meet in these places are not exactly like us, they do have the same illness. We can see in them our own struggles and glimpses of our own possibilities. Being part of a Twelve Step fellowship or other self-help group also reduces the isolation that triggers binges and maintains denial. It gives us an opportunity to observe a variety of ways to handle problems. When we don't know what to do, we have people to ask. And if they don't know either, at least we can look for answers together.

Finally, and perhaps most important, the people who have been where we are now can spot our denial and self-deception before we do. With a well-timed and gently but clearly voiced "I think there's something you're not seeing" or "Are you sure you aren't looking for an excuse to binge?" they can save us from falling into our old ways—if we are *receptive*.

In early recovery, when our self-esteem and courage may be at an all-time low, dealing with people—even supportive people— can be quite difficult. Everyone we meet may appear to be happier, healthier, and better at recovery than we are. We may be afraid to let them know that we aren't faring as well, so we clam up in their presence or have trouble listening to their advice or pretend that we are doing wonderfully. Some of us will sit with supportive people, yearning to share but saying nothing, because we can't imagine that anyone who knew the truth about us could accept us.

On the other hand, some of us do share and are overwhelmed by the support we receive. We feel so strange about it, so unworthy of it that we may even eat over it. And some of us fear being vulnerable. We decide that the people who are offering support are too much of one thing or not enough of another to truly understand us. A great many of us miss numerous opportunities to grow in our recovery by building such walls.

So *try to build bridges instead,* and be aware of the universal tendency to compare your insides to other people's outsides—to conclude that you are unworthy or they are incapable, based solely on what you can see with the naked eye. Try to suspend judgment temporarily and put yourself in a receptive frame of mind. Listen for feelings, similarities, or solutions they've found that you might try. Although everything you hear may not suit you, if you are willing to take what fits and leave the rest, you are practically guaranteed to receive what you need.

Reach Out to a Power Greater Than Yourself

The concept of relying on a power greater than ourselves to relieve our obsessions and compulsions is the mainstay of Twelve Step fellowships such as OA. Unfortunately, it is also the concept that initially steers many eating disorder sufferers away from that program. References to God, a Higher Power, and prayer convince them that OA is too religious, or some sort of cult, or simply asking them to do something they are disinclined to do—believe and put their faith in an entity they cannot perceive with their five senses.

My intent here is not to insist that you do so, but rather to briefly address a somewhat obvious point: *If our willpower alone is no match for obsessive thinking, compulsive behavior, or substances upon which our bodies have become dependent, then we will need to draw additional power from some other source.* That source can be human—a counselor, support group, or loving friend. But it also can be spiritual. We can call that spiritual source God, or our Higher Power, or our guardian angel, or the Force. We can draw strength and inspiration from it any way we choose—through prayer and meditation, reading and reflection, or the practices and traditions of organized religion.

I am best able to get quiet and listen to my Higher Power, whom I call God, while running along the ocean near my home. Something about the sand, sea, sky, and my rhythmic footfalls releases me from my earthly worries and clears a channel for more heavenly communications. Journal writing allows me to establish a similar spiritual connection. I address my writings to God, begin by describing my immediate feelings or circumstances, and then let the words spill out unedited. As my pen flows freely across the page, insights and words of encouragement more serene and sensible than my usual thought patterns appear. I am always comforted. In fact, I am comforted in simply knowing that my Higher Power is there to reach out to when sharing in a group or one-on-one seems too risky.

My faith in a gentle, loving, and forgiving God who does not want me to suffer needlessly has been my most reliable recovery safety net. It has been a well of hope, inspiration, and relief that has never run dry the way my willpower did. You may never feel this way—and that's okay. But if you do have the slightest inclination to turn to a spiritual source of strength, wisdom, and serenity, I encourage you to do so.

Abstain from the Foods and Behaviors You Can't Control

Simply put, we can't get well if we're still doing the things that make us sick. We must identify and stay away from anything that activates the addiction process. This is a purely practical matter. If we don't have the first bite of foods that have repeatedly proved to be problematic for us, we won't have the second, third, or thirty-second. Similarly, if we don't start new crash diets, the inevitable weight gain after we stop starving ourselves won't set us up for our next bout of bingeing.

Physical abstinence—refraining from compulsive eating, eating problem foods, or bingeing and purging—is to the food addict what being clean and sober is to alcoholics or drug addicts. But unlike smoking crack cocaine or drinking, eating cannot be given up completely. Food isn't optional. We must eat some of it to survive. What's more, the temptation to engage in our addictive behavior is everywhere—at breakfast, lunch, and dinner; in every convenience store, shopping mall, and banquet hall; during staff meetings, airline flights, and children's birthday parties. That makes abstinence tough to maintain once we find it—which is no mean feat to begin with. There's no consensus among experts as to what constitutes abstinent eating and little conclusive research about which foods, if any, have physically addicting properties. You could ask a dozen people about abstinence and get a dozen different answers.

My feeling on the matter is this: Generally speaking, an abstinent food plan is one that includes enough of the right foods to meet your nutritional needs and does not include any foods that have been problematic for you in the past. It should be varied, realistic, and flexible enough not to leave you feeling deprived, famished, bored, or severely limited in what you can do. On a workable food plan, you

- feel healthy
- have enough energy to meet the demands of your daily life and do not feel lethargic, fatigued, or mentally foggy
- don't spend an inordinate amount of time thinking about what you can and can't eat, counting the minutes till your next meal, or feeling as if you're starving
- are able to accommodate your natural biological tendencies rather than fighting them

Because each of us has our own unique biochemistry, life history, deeply ingrained habits, or emotional attachments to certain comfort foods, a food plan that meets the preceding criteria and works marvelously for someone else may not necessarily work for you.

For instance, even though I'm an early riser, I have never been a morning eater. The sight of anything more than a piece of fruit before 11:00 A.M. or noon makes me gag, but when my OA food sponsor told me to eat a full breakfast, I forced myself to, believing that I had to follow her every instruction to the letter.

Unfortunately, I also continued to eat more food than I'd planned for at night—which had always been the time I was hungriest. Now, whether or not night eating is right or wrong, it was what I was naturally inclined to do, and eating breakfast was not. So I switched to eating a piece of fruit in the morning and then ate the first of my meals at noon and the last at 8:30 or 9:00 at night. This worked for me. It may not work for you. The point is to find out what does.

Identify Specific Behaviors and Substances That Are Addictive for You

With the assistance of a nutritionist, eating disorder counselor, or experienced recovering overeater or bulimic, look at *what* you've been eating and its effect on you. You may find that you've been overloading your system with refined sugars, giving yourself an energy boost or emotional uplift by rapidly raising your glucose level. That triggers the release of excess insulin, which brings down the glucose level and creates the need for another sugar fix.

Or you may notice that you overeat processed wheat products like breads, cereal, and pasta. They work like anesthetics, decreasing sensitivity to pain as well as causing drowsiness and difficulty in concentrating. When they wear off, you'll want more. Many compulsive eaters and bulimics eliminate both refined sugars and processed wheat products from their food plans entirely.

Also look at your personal comfort foods—the items you reach for and end up bingeing on when you're lonely, tired, stressed, or in need of loving care. You may choose to limit the amount you eat or the circumstances under which you eat those foods.

Some of you will discover that a number of the foods you overeat actually make you ill with headaches, stomach pains, sinus or breathing problems, and a wide array of other symptoms. In some perverse way, our brains create cravings for foods that our bodies can't tolerate—and those cravings are more powerful than any interest we might have in avoiding physical discomfort. An allergist can help you identify foods in this category, which are best eliminated entirely.

When defining abstinence, we must also identify the behaviors that have repeatedly outmatched our willpower. Self-induced vomiting, laxative abuse, skipping meals and then eating almost continuously from four in the afternoon until midnight, weighing yourself many times a day, or eating in your car are just a few such behaviors you may want to curtail.

Learn to Recognize and Deal with Withdrawal Symptoms

When your body has come to depend on certain substances and you take those substances away, there's hell to pay. It's called withdrawal, and it seems that food addicts who stop consuming certain foods, primarily refined sugar or processed wheat products, can expect to go through it. Its symptoms include dizziness, chills, nausea, cravings, headaches, lethargy, and poor concentration. These will pass if you don't succumb to the urge to medicate yourself with the very substances you're trying to get out of your system.

One of the withdrawal symptoms that tends to persist long after the others have subsided is craving the foods we are no longer consuming. Cravings are natural desires intensified because they are going unfulfilled. They are most intense (and primarily biochemically induced) during the first few weeks or months of recovery. Later, they fluctuate between moderate and high intensity and are triggered by mood changes or stress. As more time passes, cravings become milder and less frequent, usually popping up in situations that remind us of our old behavior. They can take the form of

- compelling urges
- unbidden, intrusive thoughts about "off-limits" foods or old behaviors
- euphoric memories—a rose-colored-glasses view of our former behavior, in which we remember the pleasurable sensations but none of the negative consequences
- dreams of eating "forbidden" foods or of engaging in taboo behaviors, in which the images are so vivid and lifelike that we wake up virtually convinced that we actually did what we dreamed
- mentally planning a binge

People without food addictions stop cravings by satisfying them, but that's the worst thing compulsive eaters or bulimics can do. Giving in to cravings increases rather than satisfies them. Consequently, when they strike, remember that cravings are normal occurrences that anyone who has given up an addictive substance experiences. Then talk to a supportive person, go for a walk or do some other form of exercise, and remove yourself from the setting that triggered the craving. If you stop paying attention to it, the craving will go away. Once it does, don't dwell on it. Go back to what you were doing, or start something new.

Tailor Your Food Plan to Fit Your Abstinence

If you adopt a food plan that someone suggested, or in some instances, insisted, you follow, and months later you are still struggling to stick to it, consider the possibility that it is out of tune with your body's natural rhythms and biochemistry. Rather than carrying on the same old uphill battle, get some advice, make some adjustments, and give the modified version of your food plan a four- to six-week trial run. Repeat the process if necessary.

Don't Mess with Success

"The trouble with this disease is that it makes you think you don't have a disease," says Carrie, a forty-year-old OA veteran. She is struggling with physical abstinence for what she estimates to be the tenth time since getting into recovery.

"I'll go along for a while following a food plan, having clean abstinence, feeling good," Carrie says. "But then I start thinking, *Hey, this isn't so hard. I'm controlling my eating. Maybe I'm not a compulsive eater after all.* Once I get that into my head, I'm a goner. I start to cut a few things out of my food plan, thinking I'll lose weight faster. Then I'll treat myself to something I shouldn't have as a reward for eating so little the day before. Everything about my food—what I eat, how much, when, where—gets sloppier until I'm right back where I started."

As Carrie has discovered, the temptation to mess around with a good food plan can be enormous—especially if we still doubt that our food intake is truly uncontrollable. When we feel that way, we may start tinkering to prove that we're in the driver's seat, that we have the power to change our food plans.

We'll modify our eating patterns not because they're physiologically wrong for us, and not because circumstances prevented us from getting what we planned to eat, but because we felt like it or convinced ourselves we were entitled or came home exhausted and couldn't think about cooking. All we'll actually prove by flexing our self-will muscles in this manner is that we are still compulsive eaters and bulimics who, while busy fending off renewed food thoughts and cravings, are unable to control our eating—or manage our lives.

So, please, try to refrain from arbitrarily adding to or subtracting from your food plan, and make substitutions only when planned.

No One Said It Would Be Easy

Embarking on a program of recovery is a courageous, self-enhancing, potentially lifesaving act. But it isn't easy. In fact, it may be one of the most difficult things you've ever tried to do. You probably won't do it flawlessly or end your addictive behaviors on your first attempt. Be patient and persevere. A certain amount of slipping and sliding occurs in any recovery process. And lifelong connections between food and emotions simply won't be severed overnight—especially when we aren't fully aware of their existence.

Why Me?

Why did we begin to misuse food . . . become preoccupied with the size and shape of our bodies . . . turn to various substances and activities to alter our moods? No one can say with certainty—although some experts propose that the answer lies in our genes. We were born with a predisposition to overeat, they postulate, or a chemical imbalance that made us susceptible to the soothing properties of certain foods. Others suspect a glitch somewhere in our brains: a short circuit of sorts that prompts us to respond to a wide range of needs and emotions by obsessively thinking about food or compulsively feeding ourselves.

While sociologists point to the inflated value our culture places on thinness and the pressure on men and women to measure up to the standards of attractiveness depicted by the media, psychiatrists are more likely to blame psychological conflicts, some of them dating all the way back to the first year or so of our lives. Other clinicians suggest that a compulsion to overeat may be triggered later in life by circumstances that we, as children, couldn't comprehend, much less control, or from traumatic experiences that interfered with our social or psychological development. Still others claim that our compulsive behaviors are simply habits—responses we learned and practiced until they became automatic.

As far as I'm concerned, *all* of the above could be true. I believe that there is no single definitive reason for food addiction, but rather a cluster of causes. Some, such as the dramatic effect certain foods have on us, are universal. Others are unique to each individual.

The next step in our transition from addiction to recovery is to identify those factors, explore the origins of our eating disorders, and recognize the needs we've been using food or compulsive behavior to fulfill.

CHAPTER FOUR

Where Were You When They Were Handing Out Life Skills?

No matter where our eating disorders have taken us or how much we regret what we have done because of them, our compulsive behaviors were not criminal acts or random ones. When we began to use food for its mood-altering properties, dieting as a distraction, or purging as a release, *we were trying to help ourselves.* We were attempting to make ourselves feel better, to fulfill a need or fill a void or contend with circumstances that we were unable to change or control. At that moment, suppressing our unsettling emotions or directing our attention elsewhere by eating compulsively or dieting obsessively was the best, or only, coping mechanism available to us. And it worked. Time and again throughout our lives, addictive substances and behaviors came to our rescue when there seemed to be no other avenue for relief.

Long after our "cure" became an illness that made our lives more unmanageable, we continued to automatically and habitually engage in the same behaviors because, at the most fundamental level, we thought we had to. We didn't know what else to do. Even though we *consciously* hated our actions, our weight, or our lack of willpower and wanted to change it, we had *unconsciously* linked food, eating, dieting, or bingeing and purging to essential needs (safety, soothing, stability, some control over our own destinies) and vested our compulsive behavior, and in some instances, our large bodies, with the magical power to fulfill those needs.

Making Magic

Kara, thirty-one, had been struggling to curtail her compulsive eating for years when she tuned in to a TV talk show about the connection between sexual abuse and eating disorders. "Every woman on the panel sounded just like me," she remembers. Although she had been plagued by food and weight problems since childhood, her eating and her life took a dramatic turn for the worse after a date rape that occurred when she was nineteen.

Her date was a friend of her cousin's and they'd gone out twice before without him being overly pushy. His interest in stopping at his apartment between dinner and the movie they'd planned to see didn't seem odd to her. The suggestive comments he made in the elevator didn't alarm her. "I was actually sort of flattered," she admits now.

"I had just lost thirty pounds and was feeling pretty good about myself," Kara recalls. "I'd started wearing jeans and sweaters that showed off my figure instead of smock tops and baggy painter's pants that hid it, and I was definitely getting a lot of attention from guys—which I wasn't used to." For a long time afterward, Kara believed that if she had not been so inexperienced, she would have realized that her date had an ulterior motive for asking her to come up to his apartment.

When her date pulled her into an embrace and started kissing her as soon as the apartment door closed behind them, she thought nothing of it. After all, they had kissed before.

"But then things got out of hand," Kara says. "He was all over me, and when I told him to cut it out, he wouldn't. I tried to push him away, and he got furious and really rough with me." After cursing at her and calling her a tease, he pushed Kara down onto the floor and pinned her there. "I was petrified," Kara says, her voice quivering. "I didn't think I could stop him, so I just spaced out. I shut off my brain and let him do whatever he wanted." For over a decade, she would recall no details of the assault—and told no one about it.

"I tried to forget it," she says. "I wanted to block it out of my mind forever. But I never could, not completely." One particular image from that evening returned to haunt her from time to time.

"It was after midnight," Kara explains, "and I was in a subway car all by myself, but I wasn't afraid. Nothing could hurt me—because I felt like there was nothing to me. I remember staring at my reflection in the window next to me and thinking that it had more substance than I did."

In response to this feeling of complete emptiness and other aftershocks of the date rape, Kara turned to the coping strategy she had been using off and on throughout her life—numbing herself with food. When she got home, she went straight to the freezer, took out a half-gallon of ice cream, and started spooning it into her mouth as quickly as she could. "I stopped long enough to get a bag of pretzels to eat with it and went back and forth between the two. Pretzels. Ice cream. Pretzels. Ice cream. Like a zombie. My mother came into the kitchen and said my name three times before I noticed her standing there or the ice cream dribbling down my chin and pretzel crumbs all over my new sweater."

Kara's mother wanted to know what was wrong. "Why are you eating like that?" she asked. Kara didn't know. She went off to college weighing 140 pounds, returned home at the end of the school year 60 pounds heavier, and still had no idea why she was eating so much. "I wasn't even aware of how much I was eating," she says. But one thing was clear. At 200 pounds, she wasn't asked out on dates where she might have to fend off men's sexual advances; her excess weight did that for her. "I was saying no with my body because I had learned the hard way that men didn't listen to my words," Kara explains. "Of course, if you had told me that at the time, I wouldn't have believed you. I hated being overweight. I thought the only thing it did was make me miserable."

She even went on dozens of "starvation" diets to lose that weight, but she abandoned them around the same time that men who hadn't noticed her while she was fat began to show interest in her. Kara didn't see this correlation either—until the TV talk show convinced her that her overeating habit might somehow be linked to the date rape.

Kara went into therapy and began to see the tangled web she

had woven to avoid dealing with her feelings about that experience. "Right after that incident," Kara says, "I made a bunch of decisions about men, that they couldn't be trusted, that they were only after one thing—sex—and if they wanted it bad enough, nothing a woman could say was going to stop them. I *know* I told myself that I had to watch myself and protect myself when I was around them."

Compulsive eating helped her keep that vow. It squelched the anxiety she felt toward men and created a protective wall of fat around her. Although Kara "hated" her eating disorder, it also served her, giving her something meaningful and valuable that she knew no other way to obtain. And so it is for us all.

Secondary Gains

Although they may not be the same ones Kara got, almost all of us, without realizing it or planning to, receive hidden benefits from our eating disorders, which is one of the reasons they are so difficult to overcome. Until we find other methods to address the needs our eating and excess weight have been fulfilling, those needs will repeatedly draw us back into our addiction. Fortunately, substitutions can be made with relative ease when we *actually know what we've been obtaining or avoiding by eating compulsively, dieting obsessively, or bingeing and purging.* Unfortunately, most of us don't.

As young compulsive eaters or bulimics in training, we never actually told ourselves things like "Nothing I do is good enough to please my father. So I'll show him that he can't control me by eating double and triple portions at every meal." Likewise, as adult food addicts, we didn't say, "The only way I can cope with my screaming kids and unreasonable boss is to eat my way through a king-size bag of potato chips." It didn't occur to us that focusing all of our attention on our weight problem was a convenient way to avoid facing marital, financial, sexual, or loneliness problems that took more than a low-calorie diet to undo.

While we were eating compulsively, dieting obsessively, or bingeing and purging, we killed our pain before we could feel it, much less understand it. We converted complex concerns into obsessions and compulsions without recognizing what those concerns were, much less examining and making sense out of them. As a result, the connection between *what we were doing* and *why we were doing it* remained hidden from our conscious awareness. Since we can only change what we can see, we'll need to uncover that connection before we can hope to find lasting recovery.

⊱⊰

THE HIDDEN MEANINGS AND MAGICAL POWERS
WE ASSIGN TO FOOD

Those of us with eating disorders are not the only ones who attribute more meaning to food than it actually has. Virtually everyone in our culture associates food with security and celebrations of all kinds. However, we compulsive eaters or bulimics attribute *more* meanings to food under *more* circumstances and tend to use it as our *primary* or *only* means of satisfying our needs. For people without eating disorders, food is a *supplement* to their repertoire of coping strategies. For us, it is very often a *substitute* for all other ways of achieving certain goals.

To discover some of the substitutions you've made and connections that may still exist somewhere in your mind, answer the questions below.

Has food been a substitute for love? Have you eaten when the acceptance or affection you wanted from a parent, spouse, friend, or lover was not forthcoming? How often?

_____ frequently _____sometimes _____rarely _____never

Has food filled the void left by the absence of close relationships? Have you eaten when you felt lonely or like an outsider at a social gathering? How often?

_____ frequently _____sometimes _____rarely _____never

Have you nurtured yourself with food—feeding yourself when

you longed for another person's care? Were you especially prone to do that after a draining day of taking care of others? How often?

_____ frequently _____ sometimes _____ rarely _____ never

Has eating been an activity that postponed distasteful tasks or helped you face anxiety-provoking situations? Have you reached for food when a deadline was approaching or a conflict was brewing?

_____ frequently _____ sometimes _____ rarely _____ never

Was food a source of immediate gratification, especially when the road to your goals seemed full of obstacles? Have you eaten out of frustration or impatience when things didn't go the way you wanted?

_____ frequently _____ sometimes _____ rarely _____ never

Was eating an act of rebellion or resentment? Have you used it to get back at someone or prove that you weren't entirely controlled by someone who made unreasonable demands or stifled you in some other way?

_____ frequently _____ sometimes _____ rarely _____ never

Have you used food as a reward for a job well done?

_____ frequently _____ sometimes _____ rarely _____ never

. . . as consolation or solace for various losses or disappointments?

_____ frequently _____ sometimes _____ rarely _____ never

. . . as an instrument for self-punishment? After making a mistake or otherwise "misbehaving," have you overeaten and then berated yourself for it?

_____ frequently _____ sometimes _____ rarely _____ never

How has food assisted you in blocking out unacceptable emotions? How often have you eaten instead of expressing or acknowledging

FEAR?	___frequently	___sometimes	___rarely	___never
HATE?	___frequently	___sometimes	___rarely	___never
ANGER?	___frequently	___sometimes	___rarely	___never
SADNESS?	___frequently	___sometimes	___rarely	___never
ANXIETY?	___frequently	___sometimes	___rarely	___never
GUILT?	___frequently	___sometimes	___rarely	___never
SEXUAL IMPULSES?	___frequently	___sometimes	___rarely	___never

THE HIDDEN MEANINGS AND MAGICAL POWERS OF LARGE BODIES

Like food and eating, our excess pounds served a purpose in our lives, providing us with something that, despite all our protests to the contrary, we couldn't bear to lose. We let go of extra weight only to take it back because we subconsciously believed that we wouldn't be as secure or in control without it. That pattern will continue well into our recovery—unless we become more aware of the benefits we've been deriving from our much-maligned body fat. Here are a few of the most common.

Fat can be a social barrier signaling our desire to be left alone or supplying us with an excuse to avoid certain social interactions. How likely is it that you used your weight that way?

_____ very likely   _____ quite likely

_____ somewhat likely   _____ very unlikely

As it was for Kara, fat can be a protective barrier against unwanted sexual overtures, our own sexual impulses, and the guilt, shame, vulnerability, intimacy, or victimization that could result from either or both. How likely is it that you used your weight that way?

_____ very likely   _____ quite likely

_____ somewhat likely   _____ very unlikely

Fat can be a means to maintain the status quo. By telling ourselves we can't apply for a new job, date, become intimate with anyone, or embark on other endeavors until we lose some weight, we avoid new challenges and eliminate the possibility of failure. How likely is it that you used your weight that way?

_____ very likely   _____ quite likely

_____ somewhat likely   _____ very unlikely

Fat can be a symbol of independence or rebellion. With our large bodies, we are saying, "You can't push me around. I refuse to do what you want me to do or look the way you want me to look." How likely is it that you used your weight that way?

_____ very likely   _____ quite likely

_____ somewhat likely   _____ very unlikely

Fat can be a handy explanation for rejection, failure, or lack of companionship. Better to be passed over for a promotion because "society discriminates against fat people" or to be dateless on a Saturday night because "men aren't interested in women who don't look like cover girls" than because of some other deficiency. How likely is it that you used your weight that way?

_____ very likely   _____ quite likely

_____ somewhat likely   _____ very unlikely

Being fat can be a way to keep others from expecting too much of us. By taking advantage of the assumptions that fat people are lazy, undisciplined, physically unhealthy, and difficult to take seriously, we get out of anything from mowing the lawn to chairing a committee. How likely is it that you used your weight that way?

____ very likely   ____ quite likely

____ somewhat likely   ____ very unlikely

Being fat can be a form of self-punishment. Suffering from low self-esteem and years of dieting failure, we hang on to our extra-large bodies as retribution for being "rotten" or "stupid." In addition, because success, serenity, and happiness are so out of sync with our internal belief system, when we sense that things are going too well, we begin to take back weight we've lost and further punish ourselves by feeling bad about it. How likely is it that you used your weight that way?

____ very likely   ____ quite likely

____ somewhat likely   ____ very unlikely

Staying fat can be a way to avoid challenging a lifetime of magical thinking and finding out that losing weight does not automatically make us happy, healthy, successful, or loved. How likely is it that you used your weight that way?

____ very likely   ____ quite likely

____ somewhat likely   ____ very unlikely

Fat can help us project a more powerful physical presence and create the impression that we are stronger or more substantial than we might otherwise appear to be. In business as well as in personal relationships we can gain an advantage by intimidating others with our size. How likely is it that you used your weight that way?

____ very likely   ____ quite likely

____ somewhat likely   ____ very unlikely

Finally, being overweight can be a means of expressing anger and resentment, especially toward parents, spouses, or other people who put a lot of stock in physical appearances. By keeping weight on—or even adding a few more pounds— we're able to get back at those who nag us to lose weight or insinuate that we are less lovable or capable because of it. How likely is it that you used your weight that way?

_____ very likely   _____ quite likely

_____ somewhat likely   _____ very unlikely

Think about the questions you answered with "frequently," "sometimes," "very likely," or "quite likely," and in your recovery journal, jot down some specific examples of times when food, eating, or excess weight served those purposes in your life. Give particular attention to circumstances or conditions you are likely to experience again in the future.

❧

In the remainder of this chapter, you'll find a series of awareness exercises and self-tests to help you figure out some of the reasons why you came to use food and fat in the ways you've identified. I encourage you to read them all, doing those that interest you now and completing others at your leisure or in conjunction with various self-help strategies located in Part III of this book.

With each exercise, dig only as deep as you feel comfortable digging. If you aren't ready to examine something just yet, don't. You can probe further when you are ready and also redo certain exercises if previously unseen issues rise to the surface later in your recovery.

Your Psychological Inheritance

There's little doubt that life would have been a lot easier for those of us with eating disorders if we had arrived with an owner's manual at birth. Our parents could have followed the instructions in the section on "The Care and Feeding of Your New, Fragile Human Being" and spared us all sorts of pain and confusion.

We could have taken possession of our owner's manual when we were old enough to read it, and each time we found ourselves in trouble, we could have turned to a glossary of "error messages" like those found in computer software handbooks. Once we located the problem we were facing, we could have learned what we were feeling, why, and what to do about it. With that sort of information at our fingertips, we could have sailed through childhood, adolescence, and young adulthood unscathed. And we probably wouldn't have developed eating disorders.

As it was, we, like the rest of the human race, blundered along without a comprehensive handbook for living to consult. We based our perceptions of ourselves, others, and the world at large on random experiences and the examples set for us by families that bore little resemblance to the Brady Bunch or the cast of "Father Knows Best."

During our childhood, some of what we learned about ourselves, others, and living in the world was conveyed to us in subtle and seemingly benign ways—such as being gently warned away from potentially dangerous situations. When we showed an interest in trying new things or reaching out to new people, our parents or other adults may have discouraged us, sincerely believing that they were looking out for our welfare. "Don't do that. You'll hurt yourself," they said. "Don't get your hopes up. You'll be disappointed." But what we *heard* was "You can't trust yourself, or anyone else for that matter."

We also may have adopted certain unhealthy attitudes or behaviors because we were rewarded for meeting what were actually unreasonable expectations. I know I was. As far back as I can remember, grown-ups praised me for being self-sufficient. They marveled at how little attention I required. To this day my mother proudly relates how, even as a toddler, I needed so little care that she could sit me on the beach with a bucket and shovel while she socialized with her friends and, hours later, I'd still be right where she had left me, playing by myself and "not bothering anyone." I took that (and countless messages of a similar nature) to mean that I wasn't *supposed* to need attention, that a "good" person never "bothered" anyone with his or her needs.

However, most of what we learned in our childhood was learned unconsciously. As we went about the business of daily living, we took in everything that went on around us—our parents' reactions to us, the way they interacted with each other, what they or others did when they were angry or sad, how they handled conflicts and responsibilities. From our observations, we pieced together a picture of the way things were supposed to be done—and then we did things that way.

This process, which can take place completely outside our conscious awareness, had its most powerful impact on us during early childhood. For one thing, when we were young, our families were our entire world. They were all we knew, the only people with whom we could feel even remotely safe and secure. Consequently, we had a pressing need to be part of our families—and emulating our parents and siblings was one of the ways we did that. Second, as youngsters, we were empty vessels. Because we had no standard of comparison, whatever we observed and absorbed became our reality. Our minds were like fertile, as yet unplanted fields, in which any seed sown took root, flourished, and would be difficult to weed out later.

Because of our individual temperaments, birth order, the later influence of our peers, or other variables, we may not necessarily behave exactly as other family members do. In some instances, we may even have vowed never to be like them and adopted dramatically different behaviors. But in most areas of our lives, we were apt to follow the examples set for us automatically.

If we witnessed overreactions and underreactions, violence and secrecy, finger-pointing, name-calling, impatience, and little or no intimacy, we psychologically inherited at least some of those unhealthy habits and attitudes. If one or both of our parents were alcoholics, drug or sex addicts, compulsive gamblers or spenders, or workaholics, they showed us that it was possible—and quite possibly in our best interest—to use substances and activities to alter our moods or avoid unpleasant realities. We may not have picked up the same drug or activity they did, but we did pick up something.

In addition, the ideas and actions that are the mainstay of any eating disorder flourish in homes where there is an overemphasis on food, weight, and what we eat. And most of ours fit that description. At the very least, we may have been forced to clean our plates regardless of whether we were hungry or not. We were reminded that children in Appalachia were starving or that good boys and girls eat everything that's put in front of them.

Like the parents of an estimated 90 percent of all eating disorder sufferers, one or both of ours may have been obsessive weight watchers. My mother was constantly on a diet. In fact, she has yet to end a meal without saying, "I ate too much" or "I'm getting fat." And I can still recall the evening meals where my father, having restricted himself to five hundred calories during the day, would ceremoniously open a package of chocolate cupcakes and savor each morsel.

Or there may have been another food addict in the house, someone we could observe hoarding food or laxatives, marching off to the bathroom to vomit after every meal or living on lettuce leaves one week and pigging out the next. If we happened to be that person's "eating buddy," not only his or her behavior but also the conspiratorial air and sense of camaraderie that accompanied our shared binges contributed to our growing inclination to overeat.

❧

TRAITS OF CHILDHOOD MODELS

To identify some of the traits you psychologically inherited from your childhood role models, take out your recovery journal and, turning it sideways, duplicate the following chart.

69

Trait	Mom	Dad	Other Relatives	Me Today

Then pick several traits from the following list and jot down in the appropriate columns how that individual handled the emotion or circumstances in question.

ANGER
DISAPPOINTMENT
FEAR
ANXIETY
CONFLICT
STRESS
UNEXPECTED EVENTS
EATING AT MEALTIMES
EATING BETWEEN MEALS
EATING FOR REASONS OTHER THAN HUNGER
DIETING
OTHER WEIGHT-CONTROL MEASURES

In the Me Today column, note any similarities (or exactly opposite reactions) to the attitudes and behaviors exhibited by your family members.

Then, using a check mark, identify the traits or behavior patterns that you'd most like to change. To actually change them, follow the suggestions in the self-help sections that appear later in this book.

Your Addictive Self-Talk

When they were angry or preoccupied, depressed or exhausted, our parents and other influential people in our lives may have said or done things to convince us that we were incompetent, invisible, or inherently flawed. We believed them. The treatment we received may have left us feeling powerless, shameful, as if we only existed to meet others' needs. And we believed that too. If our problem with food and weight became apparent during our youth, more negative messages came our way. We were told that we had no willpower, subjected to disgusted glances at the dinner table or frustrated sighs in the dressing room of the Chubby Child department, and called pudgy, tub of lard, or blimpy. Our parents put us on diets, dragged us to psychiatrists, sent us to fat-kid camps, and accused us of being gluttons or having no pride. We took all this to heart as well.

In fact, we internalized virtually every negative message conveyed to us. We learned to see ourselves as others led us to believe they saw us and to treat ourselves as we were treated. After a while, no one had to call us weak-willed or fat. We said such things and worse to ourselves, and that negative self-talk set off the emotional uproar that triggered our obsessions and compulsions.

❧

SELF-TALK EXERCISE

To familiarize yourself with some of your self-talk, turn to your journal again, and record your answers to the following questions: What do you say to yourself when you

- make a mistake?
- overeat?
- are plagued by food thoughts?
- are faced with a new challenge?
- have an important decision to make?
- need another person's help or advice?
- wonder what someone else thinks about you?

- receive a compliment?
- are struggling with your recovery?
- have gone for any length of time without experiencing a crisis or setback?

When and from whom have you previously received similar messages? For each statement you can trace back to a specific source, jot down names or brief notes about the circumstances involved. Since all of your programming didn't originate in your family of origin, also include extended family members, teachers, peers, former lovers, and so on.

In later chapters I'll show you how to root out, combat, and revise these elements of your psychological programming. In the meantime, simply consider the possibility that because of the message-senders' own problems or the situation in which the message was conveyed, the information you received may have been wrong at the time and is, in all likelihood, unreasonable or untrue today. Then underline anything you wrote down that you are already pretty sure fits that description.

⚜

The Influence of Trying or Traumatic Experiences

Although the seeds of food addiction are sown during our childhood, many of our eating disorders lie dormant until they are awakened by a traumatic event or bumpy life transition that strains our coping resources to the limit. For Kara, the instigator was the date rape. For Marjorie, the recovering bulimic introduced in chapter 2, it was leaving home for the first time and adjusting to the academic and social pressures of college life.

In my case, over the course of six mind-boggling months, my first serious relationship with a man ended abruptly; I transferred from a small college to a large university; and my mother informed me that she was divorcing my father, a fact she wouldn't make him aware of for another three months. In the interim, and in the midst of adjusting to life at a new school, I heard via the telephone every heart-wrenching detail of my parents' married life, all the agony my mother felt about ending it, and her reluctance to tell my siblings of her decision.

Being the well-trained "responsible child," I ultimately assumed that responsibility and, once again, stuffed down my feelings with food so that I could attend to everyone else's. This resulted in an alarmingly rapid ninety-pound weight gain, and I began in earnest the downward spiral that would make my life unmanageable for the next thirteen years.

Although your circumstances may bear little or no resemblance to mine or Marjorie's or Kara's, chances are that one or several confusing or painful experiences that occurred during your adolescence or young adulthood also played a major role in the development of your eating disorder. These sorts of experiences include the following:

- The loss of a loved one through death, divorce, abandonment, or breakup of an intimate relationship.
- The loss of status as a result of financial setbacks, disabling injuries or illnesses, or being demoted, laid off, or fired from a job.
- The loss of ideals or dreams, such as discovering that positions in your chosen field aren't waiting for you when you graduate from college, that your marriage or career isn't all you'd hoped it would be, that you can't have children, or that you won't in the foreseeable future be able to match the standard of living your parents had.
- Rejection by relatives, peers, lovers, employers, or social clubs.
- Social isolation (moving to a new city where you know no one, working in a hostile environment, or remaining single when more and more of your friends are getting married).
- Early sexual experiences, particularly those that left you feeling unattractive, inadequate, ashamed, or used. (Positive ones can be problematic as well, especially if you have previously received mixed or negative messages about exploring and enjoying your sexuality.)

- Life transitions and new challenges, such as puberty and the bodily changes that accompany it, trying to fit into a peer group, intensified academic pressure or competition for athletic scholarships, separating from your parents and living on your own, entering the work force, marriage, parenthood, job promotions, geographic relocation, or other tasks of adolescence and young adulthood.

- Traumatic events that shatter our sense of security, dignity, uniqueness, or personal power, such as accidents, floods, earthquakes, fires, and other situations that were truly beyond our control; being physically, emotionally, or sexually abused, being mugged, robbed, or raped, or otherwise victimized or treated as an object.

Because the human mind is geared to protect us from anything it perceives to be more than we can handle, in the immediate aftermath of trying or traumatic experiences our psyches may automatically shut down our emotions and numb our awareness. As I noted in chapter 1, this denial or retreat from reality is a natural reaction that provides temporary relief and helps us get by until we've regained our equilibrium and are ready to adapt to the changes in our lives. However, many of us, due to our backgrounds and habit of using food and compulsive behavior as a cure-all, never developed the coping resources that this sort of adaptation requires. Instead of learning, growing, and moving on, we got stuck.

⚜

LOOKING THROUGH OLD FILES

How many of the circumstances I've just described have you encountered? After referring to my list, think back over your history, and in your recovery journal, list the notable trials, tribulations, difficult transitions, and traumas you've experienced over the course of your lifetime. Don't exclude things that seem minor in retrospect. Events you would take in stride today may have indeed turned your world upside down when you were six or ten or twenty. Any upset you can still recall, no matter how small, is probably significant.

How did those events affect you at the time they occurred? Using a one through five scale, with one being "no big deal" and five being "devastation," rate the impact each experience had on you.

What *lasting* effect have they had on you? In the aftermath of trying or traumatic events, we tend to draw conclusions about ourselves and other people that have the potential to influence our behavior for years to come. Kara's decisions about men are a good example of this.

So was the conclusion I came to when my first boyfriend dumped me for a woman who wasn't spending her summer at a camp for disadvantaged children five hundred miles away from him the way I was. He wanted someone who would "be there" for him when he needed her, he explained. Doing what was important to *me* led to rejection, I decided, and coupled with the "don't be needy" message that came through loud and clear during my childhood, that assumption paved the way for years of giving everything I had to others and then gratifying my own needs with food.

On another page in your recovery journal, list some of the judgments, assumptions, or vows you think you may have made in the aftermath of events you rated three or above. Also note any attitudes or beliefs that seemed to change or become more pronounced after those incidents. Finally, go back over your original list and check any experience that was followed by a change in your eating or dieting behavior (for example, more compulsive eating, more obsessive thinking about your weight, a switch to bingeing and purging, saying to hell with your latest diet or starting a new one).

If you responded to any of your trying or traumatic events by ingesting mood-altering substances or engaging in addictive behavior, your memory bank is apt to have files overflowing with unresolved feelings, faulty perceptions, fears, or avoidance patterns.

At some point, to prevent recurrences of your eating disorder once you've begun to overcome it, you'll need to go through those files, deleting misinformation, replacing it with attitudes that support your recovery, and adopting new methods for fulfilling your needs. You can do that at any point in the recovery process—although I recommend that you work on giving up your addictive behaviors and solidifying your physical recovery first.

PART II

PHYSICAL RECOVERY

CHAPTER FIVE

Abstinence Protection

The initial phase of the recovery process, with its emphasis on physical abstinence, is designed to eliminate an old, self-defeating habit by creating a new one—abstinent living. If all goes well, refraining from our addictive behaviors becomes second nature—something that is easier and more comfortable to do than not to do. Until that day arrives, however, it is our responsibility to do everything we can to strengthen our new habit and do as little as possible to undermine it.

Abstaining from compulsive behavior is difficult and in many ways more difficult for eating disorder sufferers than for alcoholics or drug addicts. Not only must we face our nemesis at every meal, but we generally turned to our mood-altering substances and activities at a much earlier age than other addicts. We used them to fulfill a wider range of needs and tend to feel completely lost without them. Time and again—and even more so after the symptoms of our disease are no longer visible—we will wonder if staying abstinent or sticking to a program of recovery is really worth the effort it requires.

That's why there has to be more to physical recovery than simply figuring out what we will or won't eat and resolving to follow through with those plans. *We also need to construct safety nets to prevent us from falling back into our old habits.* Here's how.

Make Your Recovery Your Top Priority

"My *top* priority!" you may gasp. "Above my children, my spouse, my career, my Wednesday night yoga class?" Yes, above all those—although you need not neglect any of them. Making recovery your top priority simply means not allowing your other obligations to take you away from what you need to do to overcome your eating disorders.

Although this involves a certain amount of advance planning and lost spontaneity, that price is not nearly as high as the one we paid when we were in the grips of our food addiction. *Occasionally*, the dedication it takes to recover may seem as extreme, even as obsessive as our old addictive behavior, but the lengths we go to in order to find abstinence and get into recovery are necessary—at this point in the process. Later, as we work through the issues that contributed to our eating disorder and learn new coping skills, we can become more flexible. Moreover, making recovery our top priority is not really as limiting as we might think. Once we get the hang of it, we can lead full lives while still respecting our disease and attending to our abstinence.

You can start by *reorganizing your schedule, making room for any activities your personal program of recovery requires.* Commit yourself to a certain level of recovery-oriented activity, such as meetings, therapy, reading, meditation, and exercise. Then plan your days with that in mind. Actually schedule the tasks you must do to nourish yourself and sustain your physical abstinence. Give yourself time to prepare abstinent meals, sit down to eat them, reflect on your day, and talk with supportive people. This time won't be as difficult to find as you might think. Most of it will come from the time you used to spend eating, going on food runs, purging, replacing the food you'd eaten, thinking up excuses for your actions, or sleeping off your binges.

Take care to plan a realistic schedule: one that is active but not jam-packed, and one that is skewed toward recovery activities but not neglectful of other responsibilities. Then stick to it as closely as you can. Yes, unforeseen problems or opportunities will arise. That's the way life is—but also the way excuses are made. Try not to sacrifice your top-priority activities—the ones that serve your recovery—for anything but pressing obligations or emergencies.

Prepare a Food Plan and Find a Mentor

While developing new patterns, we need to keep everything concerning food as conscious as possible. Food planning enables us to do that. We figure out what we'll eat during a given day and write it down. Then, before we put anything in our mouths, we can ask ourselves, "Is this on my food plan?" If it isn't, we aren't to eat it. But even if we do, we'll be consciously aware of the choice we made—as opposed to taking an automatic action that we look back on in disgust and dismay.

Food planning also offers relief from obsessive food thoughts. Because our food decisions for the day have been made, we don't have to fret over what we'll eat at our next meal and are less likely to trigger cravings or compulsions by running sample menus through our minds.

Because it's normal for newly recovering individuals to start out being too rigid or to try to get away with something very loose, unwittingly setting themselves up for the same failures they experienced when dieting, it is also useful to be supervised during early recovery. Supervision, however, doesn't mean having someone smack your hand with a ruler if you reach for an "illegal" food.

Supervision means that there is someone in your life who is knowledgeable about eating disorders and willing to help you make food choices or stick to your food plan. Whether you read your food plan to a friend or an OA sponsor over the phone each morning, go over it each week with a counselor, or are walked through it during inpatient treatment, telling someone what you are going to eat and knowing that you will be asked to report back on what you actually ate will keep you honest.

That person also can offer you the guidance and support to continue on a still-unfamiliar course. Be careful about projecting images onto him or her, however. Your mentor is neither a police officer laying down laws that you'll grow to resent nor the loving, all-knowing parent, spouse, or friend you never had. Your support person won't always be right or available when you call, and at some point you'll part company.

Supervision and writing out food plans need not go on indefinitely. You can choose to discontinue both once you have grown accustomed to being abstinent and feel ready to let go.

Take Steps to Combat Denial

As I've mentioned, eating disorders are so cunning, baffling, and powerful because they are accompanied by a built-in defense system that blinds us to their existence, deludes us about what they're doing to us, and can lure us back into habits we thought we'd discarded. We advance on one front and admit that we have a chronic, progressive, addictive disease, then retreat on another and downplay the seriousness of our disorder as well as the damage it has done to us and those around us.

Okay, we think, *something's really wrong here, but is it really that bad?* Then we look for proof that it isn't, often finding it by "comparing out"—listing all the ways we differ from other compulsive overeaters or bulimics and using the items on that list as an argument against wholeheartedly pursuing recovery. We may notice people whose symptoms and problems are worse than our own and conclude that we aren't sick enough to need the same recovery program they do.

Or we may point to the ways recovering men and women differ from us in age, economic status, education, or other background traits; we then disregard the characteristics we share and focus instead on the ones we don't have in common. As long as we can find one facet of ourselves or our behavior that distinguishes us from our fellow eating disorder sufferers and convince ourselves that it could mean we really aren't food-addicted, we can avoid committing ourselves fully to the recovery process.

Others among us take a more intellectual approach and reject any recovery practices that can be refuted by "scientific" research or time-honored therapies such as psychoanalysis. "There's no conclusive proof that refined sugar is addicting," we say and continue to eat foods containing it even though we have personal proof that they trigger binges and make us lethargic or irritable.

Or we find one aspect of the recovery process that does not fit our values and life-style exactly and dismiss an entire approach because of it. *Those OA people are too religious*, we think at the first mention of a Higher Power, and we don't stick around to discover what else they might have to offer us.

No matter how we go about it, we're looking for an escape hatch, a way to get out of doing all of what we're being told we must do. Recovery seems too difficult, too slow-moving or time-consuming, too much of a threat to the status quo. And so our psyches try to convince us that *we* don't have to recover in that way. *"You're* a special case," says the little psychological defense minister in our head. *"You* can do this *your* way. Never mind that your way was what brought you to your knees. Forget all the times you did the same thing and got the same disastrous results. Go ahead and try some controlled eating, some bingeing and purging in moderation. It'll work this time, trust me."

Seeing that con job on paper, it's tough to believe that we'd fall for it, even subconsciously. But we do—and not only when we are in the throes of our eating disorder. Many of us are especially susceptible to a bout of "terminal uniqueness" after a stretch of relatively serene, abstinent living. As Ronald L. Rogers and Chandler Scott McMillin, authors of *Relapse Traps* (Bantam, 1992), put it, "While your disease is in check, it's remarkably easy to forget what life was like when it wasn't."

Combating Denial

Combating denial is a near-constant challenge during early recovery. And cold, hard facts about the true nature of our disease are the best weapons against it. So go on a fact-finding mission.

Learn as much as you can about food addiction, compulsive overeating, and bulimia and how to recover from them. Know why (1) diets don't work, (2) thin isn't well, and (3) willpower is no match for obsessions and compulsive behavior, as well as (4) how eating disorders compare to alcoholism and other addictions. Be able to define (*a*) obsession, (*b*) compulsion, (*c*) physical and psychological dependency, and (*d*) loss of control over amount, frequency, and duration of addictive behavior. Read books and pamphlets. Write on each topic in your recovery journal. Discuss your understanding of them with other recovering individuals.

Review in detail your personal history of compulsive eating, obsessive dieting, or bingeing and purging. Identify your own symptoms and acknowledge how each of the characteristics listed in the preceding paragraph manifested itself in your life while you were actively involved in your eating disorder. If you haven't already done so, complete the exercises in chapters 1 and 2. Then dig deeper or reinforce what you already know by doing the following:

- jotting down several personal experiences of willpower failing to prevent compulsive behavior.
- identifying a dozen or so ways that your eating or bingeing and purging resembles an alcoholic's drinking.
- keeping a running list titled "How I Know I Have a Chronic, Progressive, Potentially Fatal Eating Disorder and Must Abstain." Add to it each time you learn something new about yourself and your eating disorder.
- copying some of your list items onto Post-its or index cards and placing them in strategic locations—your purse, wallet, glove compartment, top desk drawer, night table, and so on. Consult them whenever you begin to doubt that you really are a compulsive eater or bulimic and must abstain.

Write out, in every gory detail, your experience of hitting bottom. Describe every element of the incident that marked your lowest low, every feeling, every horrible judgment you bestowed upon yourself, every morsel you swallowed during your last binge, every nuance of a moment in your life that you never, ever want to repeat. Hang on to this journal entry. Reread it from time to time. Make copies of it to carry with you and, when you hit a rough spot, review it to remind yourself of where you could end up if you give in to the temptation to overeat.

Then, take an even closer look at what you have to look forward to if you return to your old habits. There are only three destinations to which an eating disorder can lead you: (1) recovery, (2) death, or (3) insanity. The first two have been discussed from several angles already, but what about the third? Can compulsive eating, obsessive dieting, or bulimia actually land you in a psychiatric hospital or make you too mentally confused to function on a daily basis? Absolutely. Food addicts are prime candidates for depression, panic disorder, and obsessive-compulsive disorder (OCD). Many get their first professional attention following suicide attempts or panic attacks.

What's more, if we expand our perception of insanity to include the sheer lunacy of some of our thoughts and actions—not to mention the ever-increasing unmanageability of our lives—it becomes clear that we were well on our way to that state long before any psychiatric diagnosis could be applied to us. Who else but lunatics would

- keep track of the convenience stores where they purchased their binge food and, fearing that the clerk would remember them and know that they'd eaten it all in one night, make sure not to visit the same store two days in row;
- bury leftover chocolate cake in the bottom of a trash can so they won't eat it but later retrieve and consume it;
- drive more than one hundred miles to enroll in a liquid diet program rather than attend any of the five nearer programs they'd already been in and bombed out of?

Take some time to consider the two alternatives to recovery—insanity and death—and in your recovery journal, describe where on either or both of those roads you could be a year, two years, and five years from now if you resumed your old eating, dieting, bingeing, or purging habits.

Finally, learn to catch yourself before you fall for the same old excuses, rationalizations, and justifications for overeating or bingeing and purging. Get to know your particular brand of mental poison by identifying the defenses you used in the past.

Types of Denial
After reading the following definitions and examples of different types of denial, write about the ones you've employed, being as

specific as possible about what you said or did, when, under what circumstances and so on.

BASIC DENIAL—believing that *there is no problem* even when faced with tangible evidence to the contrary.

EXAMPLES: Saying, "I don't know what you're talking about. Everything's fine"; being convinced that you're eating normal portions when they're actually extra-large; forgetting half or more of what you ate during a given day and then not being able to understand why you aren't losing weight.

MINIMIZING—insisting that there *may* be a problem, but it's not as bad as everyone else seems to think it is.

EXAMPLES: Saying, "Sure, I've been putting on a little weight lately, but I'll take it off in no time once I start jogging again," or "I know taking laxatives and diuretics isn't good for me, but it could be worse. I could be vomiting three times a day the way so-and-so does."

BLAMING—maintaining that if there is a problem, you aren't responsible for it—someone or something else is.

EXAMPLES: "You'd overeat too if you had my spouse (kids, stressful job, genetic makeup, or traumatic childhood)," or "People are always pushing food on you, and they get offended if you turn them down."

RATIONALIZING—coming up with an infinite number of excuses and explanations to justify your behavior and its repercussions.

EXAMPLES: After ordering an extra-large pizza and eating it all yourself, you explain away your actions by telling yourself you were too tired to cook, upset over an argument with your best friend, are entitled to it after a hard day's work, or are starting a strict diet tomorrow.

INTELLECTUALIZING—focusing on intellectual theories and broad generalizations about your behavior to avoid feeling its emotional impact.

> EXAMPLES: "Everybody puts on weight when they're going through some sort of transition," or "It's a well-known fact that people don't change until they're psychologically ready to," or "There's no conclusive evidence that sugar 'highs' actually exist."

DIVERSIONS—changing the subject or turning it back on the person who raised it.

> EXAMPLES: "You could stand to lose a few pounds yourself, you know" or "Don't you have anything better to do than watch what I eat?"

HOSTILITY—becoming angry, sullenly silent, or verbally abusive when confronted with your problematic behavior.

Make the Most of Your Progress

Armed with this information, you'll be able to notice that your psyche's up to its old self-deceptive tricks *before* they can undermine your recovery. Plan to add to the list periodically as well.

More "slippery" thought patterns will emerge as your recovery progresses. In fact, the longer you manage to stay away from your binge foods and refrain from your compulsive behavior, the more insistent and ingenious your psyche's arguments may get. But you don't have to succumb to them by overeating, eating off-limits foods, or bingeing and purging. You can distract yourself instead.

Make a list of "connection breakers." Identify activities other than your compulsive behaviors that you can do the next time you notice that old mental poison seeping into your system. These relatively brief, pleasurable, productive, or essential activities can run the gamut from ironing to making a phone call, polishing your fingernails to listening to your favorite audiotape.

Physical diversions such as brisk walks or pedaling hard on your stationary bicycle are excellent connection breakers, as are mental challenges such as working on a crossword puzzle or balancing your checkbook. Cleaning out the linen closet or a desk drawer may not be fun, but you get the added bonus of a sense of accomplishment when you're done.

Make this list long and pack it with things you've meant to try or wished you had time for. Now you do. When food thoughts pop into your head or you start to con yourself into an old behavior (and simply sticking with whatever you had been doing isn't working), check your list, pick an activity, and give it your full attention for ten to fifteen minutes. Repeat if need be.

Try sharing your poisonous thoughts and feelings with someone else or writing about them. Before you act on the urge to eat, ask yourself: *What am I looking for right now? Will I really find it in the refrigerator, pantry, at a fast food restaurant? Or Why do I feel like eating right now? Am I physically hungry or is something else triggering my desire?* Then, contact a support person and discuss the matter, or, as spontaneously as possible, respond to those questions in writing. Don't concern yourself with finding the right or most logical answer. Just write. After several answers have come to you, one will strike you as closest to the truth.

Having put your thoughts down on paper, you'll usually see what you really need or want to do, such as talk your fears over with your spouse, lay down the law to your rebellious fourteen-year-old son, apologize to the secretary you snapped at, or reward yourself for having made it through a stressful situation. Having uncovered this information, you are in a position to deal with the situation instead of eating over it—*although that won't always be the choice you make.*

People's experiences in recovery vary greatly. However, I've rarely seen anyone catch on immediately and never look back. While I don't subscribe to the theory that relapse is *part* of recovery and everyone *must* go through it, many of us do fall off the wagon at least once. Others struggle from the outset, finding it practically impossible to discontinue old habits for more than a day or so—despite a sincere and often desperate desire to do so.

Fortunately, we learn and grow from our success and our failures. In terms of awareness and the ability to conduct ourselves differently in the future, *any* step, regardless of its immediate outcome, is a positive action. Even so, it's in your best interest to acquaint yourself with some of the factors that tend to cause relapses in early recovery. After all, there's no sense in tripping over things you could walk around if you knew they were there. In the next chapter, I'll point out some of those pitfalls—and show you how to avoid them.

Chapter Six

Relapse Prevention:
Avoiding the Pitfalls of Early Recovery

Fourteen months after my near-fatal gallbladder surgery, I finally admitted that I was powerless over my compulsive eating and that my life had become unmanageable. By then I had gained back sixty of the one hundred pounds I'd paid such a high physical and financial price to lose, and my weight was hovering around the two-hundred-pound mark.

Yet, I honestly wouldn't have cared if I'd never lost another ounce. I was sick and tired of being on the eating/dieting merry-go-round. I wanted to stop the downward spiral of my life, come out of isolation, and feel something about myself other than self-loathing and disgust. *Yes*, I thought, as a friend talked to me about her experiences in OA, *I'll go to any length to trade in this miserable existence for a real life.*

With that potential exchange in mind, I embarked upon a program of recovery, determined to get it right. For months, I worked my program so religiously that if there had been a "Miss OA" pageant, I would have won it. What I didn't realize until much later was that I *did* expect a reward for my efforts—to live happily ever after with no self-doubt or problems.

I was in for a rude awakening. It came during a five-day trip to my brother's home, where my mother and stepfather were also staying. I can't say exactly when the pink cloud on which I'd been floating was punctured or what specifically brought me crashing back down to earth. It could have been the toothache that started the day I arrived or the Christmas goodies that seemed to be everywhere. I know my brother's habit of getting home two hours after he said he would (and fifteen minutes before we had to be someplace else) irritated me to no end.

I can definitely recall the feeling of déjà vu during every meal we ate around my brother's dining room table—which just happened to be the same table we'd eaten at as kids. While my mother took care of "one last little thing" in the kitchen, my brother's repartee became more sarcastic and insulting. Although I'd matured enough to no longer run from the table in tears, his well-aimed barbs hit one sore spot after another, stirring up memories and emotions I was unprepared to face. Being the out-of-towner at a half-dozen holiday parties crowded with people who all knew each other had a similar effect.

Loneliness, feeling like a misfit, being mateless, playing therapist to everyone I knew—indeed, every personal matter that I hadn't paid attention to since I began devoting myself to physical recovery—came roaring to the surface during that vacation. All contributed to my downfall.

Before Christmas Day was more than a few hours old, I was into the star- and stocking-shaped sugar cookies and the chocolate kisses and handfuls of other confections. They made me feel nauseated, dizzy, "drunk" on sugar. But I didn't stop eating them—or lasagna, pretzels, sandwiches on white bread with tons of mayonnaise, and countless other items I hadn't touched since walking into my first OA meeting. It would be quite some time before I was able to turn down those binge foods again. I had lost my abstinence and spent the next seven months in relapse.

Common Triggers to Relapse

A *relapse* is a return to addictive attitudes and behaviors after a period of abstinence. Unlike a *slip*, a single episode of compulsive behavior, or a *backslide*, a struggle with food thoughts, physical cravings, or emotional issues you had believed you were done with, a relapse is marked by the reemergence of your eating disorder in all its glory—the obsessions, compulsions, loss of control, attempts at denial, and so on.

Some recovery experts consider relapse a necessary evil that can't be avoided. Many recovering individuals see it as their worst nightmare and run themselves ragged trying to avoid it. I tend to look at it as a powerful teacher offering a potent, if painful, refresher course on our disease. Once we're done with it, our understanding of and commitment to recovery are likely to be stronger than ever before. The course is optional, however. We also learn and grow by staying on the road to recovery and negotiating the twists, turns, and obstacles we encounter along the way.

From a physical standpoint, a relapse can be triggered by as little as one bite of a binge food. However, trouble usually starts before then, with misconceptions or faulty decisions made during emotional moments. These triggers are probably as numerous as the excuses and rationalizations we once used to deny the existence of our eating disorders. Here are a few of the most common:

- Trigger #1: Bringing our old diet mentality with us into recovery.
- Trigger #2: Unrealistic expectations of the recovery process.
- Trigger #3: Perfectionism.
- Trigger #4: "Slippery" people, places, and things.
- Trigger #5: Ongoing problems that we've been known to eat over in the past.
- Trigger #6: Overconcern for the welfare of others and a tendency to pay more attention to their needs and problems than our own.
- Trigger #7: Measuring our progress by comparing it to someone else's.

Trigger #1: Bringing Our Old Diet Mentality with Us into Recovery

In its most obvious form, this trigger involves treating a program of recovery as if it were just another diet plan and embarking on it with quick weight loss as our primary—or only—goal. We might, for instance, join OA six weeks before our high school reunion or three months before swimsuit season and think of it as "Weight Watchers with religion." But we'll tire of it soon enough. Since there are easier ways to diet, people who want to do only that don't stay in recovery programs for long.

The more subtle but equally self-defeating version of this trigger involves working a recovery program, but thinking we'll be able to stop working it at some point, generally when we have reached a certain weight and maintained it for a while. Taking a "one day at a time *for the time being*" approach to recovery, we may try to speed up the process and move up the date we'll be done with it by choosing a very rigid, restrictive food plan—quite like the diets we've been on in the past. As a result, we feel deprived and often physically hungry most of the time. We can barely make it from one meal to the next and may spend as much time thinking about what, how much, and when we can eat as we ever did in the past.

We hold on to our abstinence with the sort of terrified, white-knuckled death grip that a passenger with a fear of flying might have on the armrests while the plane circles the airport in a thunderstorm. Sooner or later, the pressure gets to us. We cheat a little, then a lot, and finally—as we did with all the diets that preceded abstinence—we jump ship altogether and dive right back into our old habits.

Even those of us who are quite certain that weight loss is not our main purpose for being in a recovery program may bring a hidden agenda with us—most notably, the belief that someday we'll regain control over our compulsions and be able to eat like normal people. We keep this idea tucked away in the back of our minds, seek out scientific evidence to support it, and periodically conduct our own research, testing out foods or behaviors to see what we can get away with. Each seemingly successful experiment convinces us to experiment a little more. Before we know it, we're right back where we started—up to our ears in an eating disorder that we are still powerless to control.

If we're white-knuckling it or experimenting, we haven't fully accepted that powerlessness. We aren't completely convinced that we have a chronic, progressive, addictive, and potentially fatal disease. We still believe that if we just try hard enough or find the right thing to try, we'll be able to control our food intake, weight, or compulsive behaviors. If you think that's the case for you, go back and reread chapters 1 and 2. Review or redo the exercises there. You may have to do this several times over the course of your recovery, because it really is difficult to accept the true and long-lasting nature of your eating disorder.

It also helps, as various recovery experts have noted, to narrow our focus to a single day and commit ourselves to do whatever it takes to recover *for that day*. Things we can't imagine ourselves doing for a lifetime can be followed for twenty-four hours. When developing a food plan, however, it's worthwhile to take some time to think about the long haul as well.

Try to come up with a food plan that you could follow forever *if you had to*. Ask yourself, *If push came to shove and there were no other eating options available to me, could I eat like this indefinitely? Would I be willing to follow this sort of food plan not only for the time being but also for one day at a time for the rest of my days?* An affirmative answer does not commit you to actually using that food plan for the remainder of your life, but knowing that you could— along with accepting your powerlessness—reduces the need to white-knuckle it and the temptation to experiment.

Trigger #2: Unrealistic Expectations of the Recovery Process
Those of us who enter recovery with the gung ho, follow-all-the-rules-and-get-it-right-on-the-first-try attitude that I had are particularly susceptible to this trigger. We become abstinent right away and feel proud of and a little high on our success. We quickly establish new rituals and routines and are comforted by them. We see visible results, receive pats on the back, and have people to talk to, places to go, and things to do whenever we get anxious. That feels wonderful. In fact, life seems so terrific from that pink cloud of early recovery euphoria that we can't imagine anything toppling us from it.

Not until we encounter circumstances we've never handled without using food to alter our mood or dieting to distract us does it occur to us that some things still might be too much for us. That's when we crash and learn that nothing—no substance, activity, recovery program, ritual, or spiritual practice—removes every source of conflict from our lives, especially if we aren't making an effort to resolve those problems. The happily-ever-after we believed we'd earned by working hard at physical recovery won't be immediately forthcoming. The shattering of that illusion can seriously threaten our commitment to recovery. After all, if life is still going to be unmanageable, why bother?

If you don't want this trigger to lead to a relapse, know why *you* bother. Review your writings on the past and potential consequences of food addiction and your eating disorder. The wellness exercises at the end of chapter 7 also should help.

If you're up on that pink cloud right now, enjoy the ride but realize that you'll come down to earth eventually. Prepare for an easier landing by toning down your expectations. Listen carefully as other people talk about their experiences in early recovery. Ask them about the rough spots they encountered. Read about the ups and downs of recovering individuals in personal story books such as Heidi Waldrop's *Showing Up for Life* (Hazelden Educational Materials, 1990) or Eliot Alexander's *Sick and Tired of Being Fat* (Hazelden Educational Materials, 1991). Know that you could go through some of the same peaks and valleys yourself. Also, start using the strategies found in this book's self-help sections to help you handle situations that being in recovery doesn't automatically reconcile.

Trigger #3: Perfectionism

Like the other two, this trigger is linked to our past attitudes and actions. Back in our obsessive dieting days, perfection was the only standard of success we would accept. Consuming one morsel more than we were allowed ruined an entire day of dieting. Since we had blown it already, we went all out. The next day we would compensate for our lapse by restricting our food intake even more than we had the day before, which made the diet more difficult to follow and increased our chances of slipping again. Well, the same thing can happen in recovery—not only with food, but with every other aspect of our program.

Perfectionism is part of many food addicts' basic psychological programming. It says, "Everything you do, indeed, everything about you, must be complete and flawless in all respects. Anything less is unacceptable, a cause for guilt, shame, and self-punishment. Mistakes are mortal sins, and the only way to redeem yourself is to try again with more diligence than before."

Unfortunately, because the standards that perfectionists expect of themselves are unrealistic, trying harder doesn't lead to success. It generates frustration, low self-esteem, a tendency to avoid situations in which success is not guaranteed, and a paralyzing fear of making mistakes—all of which provide fertile ground for growing an addiction.

As perfectionists, we tend to see ourselves in all-or-nothing terms. We are heroes or goats, flawless performers or complete failures. In the grandiose glare of perfectionistic thinking, excellence isn't good enough, and being ordinary is a fate worse than death. If we aren't the very best, we are nothing.

That attitude is the enemy of abstinence. If we expect too much of ourselves, we are going to fall short of that expectation. And if we react by setting a higher, more stringent expectation, we are going to fail again. Not only will that all-too-familiar sense of failure and inadequacy trigger thoughts of eating or actual food cravings, but if we fail in our own eyes often enough, we run the risk of giving up on recovery entirely.

In an effort to appear flawless, we may try to conceal our slips or insecurities from people who could help us if they knew where we hurt. And we'll berate ourselves unmercifully each time we make the slightest mistake, losing sight of the progress we've made up to that point, our positive attributes, and our motivation to recover.

The AA slogan Easy Does It was coined for a reason. It's tough enough to make it through early recovery without a relapse. Why make it more difficult? When you embark upon a program of recovery, leave your perfectionism at the door. Use it to make perfect hospital corners on your bed or add up figures perfectly, but where abstinence is concerned, just try being consistent.

Slow down. No one grasps, much less adopts, a whole new way

of eating and relating to food overnight. You don't have to tackle everything at once. Set interim goals for yourself—to get through the awards banquet without eating any rolls or dessert, to make a phone call instead of reaching for a snack, to get to your therapy appointment each week. Give yourself credit for each step, no matter how small. The steps add up and help you maintain the positive frame of mind you need to make more progress.

If, after several tries, you find that you are unable to meet some standard, don't automatically try, try again. Consider the possibility that you're aiming too high or expecting an unrealistic result, and lower that standard to an achievable level. This may mean that you stop weighing and measuring food portions for a while and instead try to eat three moderate meals a day, or that you cut back to a meeting a week plus therapy rather than trying to wedge three weekly meetings into your busy schedule. Once you've experienced some success at that new level, you can shoot for a higher goal—if you still think that's necessary. In many instances, you'll find that it's not.

Trigger #4: "Slippery" People, Places, and Things

Holiday dinners with the whole family gathered round . . . cocktail hour buffets at trade shows and sales conferences . . . the hour before bedtime when we and our binge buddies used to raid the refrigerator . . . passing a doughnut shop or Mom's kitchen . . . being with your mother, the boss, a still-bingeing-and-purging ex-college roommate . . . these are a few examples of the sorts of situations that used to set off our obsessions and compulsions—and still could. What are some of yours?

♣

ASSESSING THE RISK

Turn to a clean page in your recovery journal and start listing the following:

- *Environments* conducive to overeating or obsessing about food, weight, and so on, such as all-you-can-eat buffets, your parents' biweekly backyard barbecues, lunching with your thin-as-a-reed, always-on-a-diet sister-in-law, picking up a magazine with the words "Foolproof diet: Lose ten pounds the first week" on the cover.

- *Events* that triggered binges or cravings, such as bad blind dates, good ones when the guy didn't call again, work deadlines or presentations, tests.

- *Other compulsive eaters, binge buddies, and excuse providers,* such as people whose rejection, criticism, perfectionism, nonacceptance, or suggestions that "a little bit won't hurt" gave you what you felt was a perfectly good reason to binge and purge or overeat.

- *Traditional eating occasions,* such as Thanksgiving, Christmas, birthdays, weddings, power lunches, vacations, awards banquets.

- *Any other people, places, or things* that used to set off your addictive behavior.

Once your list is made, rate each item on a one-to-five scale, with five being the greatest potential threat to your continued recovery.

For any item with a rating of three or above, ask yourself: "Do I really have to put myself into or remain in this high-risk situation?" If not, you may need to avoid that situation entirely, as well as see some people less often and others not at all, at least until your abstinence is strong enough to withstand temptations you couldn't resist in the past.

If the potentially troublesome person, place, or thing cannot be avoided, devise—with the assistance of an OA sponsor, support group member, or professional counselor—a plan to minimize the risk and protect your abstinence. Find other ways to make special occasions special. Arrange to get some extra moral support via the telephone or by having another recovering person or someone who encourages your recovery attend an event with you.

Call ahead to order appropriate meals on airlines or find

out in advance what will be served at an awards banquet. If you feel you can handle it, create a for-this-day-only food plan that gives you a little more leeway, such as larger portions, greater variety of foods, and more flexible mealtime, without giving you permission to flagrantly overindulge or indulge at all in your known binge foods.

⚜

Trigger #5: Ongoing Problems That We've Been Known to Eat Over in the Past

Over the years, our control-freak spouses, rebellious teenagers, overbearing in-laws, or unappreciative bosses have provided us with an endless supply of excuses to overeat or binge and purge. They won't stop now, so don't expect them to. List these "threats" too. Then use your support network and this book's self-help sections to come up with alternative methods for dealing with conflicts, anger, resentment, rejection, and other relationship uproars.

And remember, unless the people in your life tie you down and force-feed you, they cannot make you overeat, eat foods that cause problems for you, or engage in compulsive behaviors.

Trigger #6: Overconcern for the Welfare of Others and a Tendency To Pay More Attention to Their Needs and Problems Than Our Own

This can be a convenient way of not looking at our own lives and an easy out when life without food fixes or dieting distractions seems too difficult. *They really need me right now*, we think, and put our abstinence, meetings, and therapy on the back burner until their crisis passes.

Recovery requires what initially seems like selfishness but is actually self-concern. It asks us to start saying, "I am important. I do care about myself, and my recovery is my top priority today." Try reviewing the section on priorities in the previous chapter and following the suggestions for establishing boundaries in chapter 12.

Trigger #7: Measuring Our Progress by Comparing It to Someone Else's

We compulsive eaters and bulimics tend to be black-and-white thinkers. We don't like the gray areas. But recovery is full of them and can leave us in a constant quandary about our own status. *Am I doing this right?* we wonder. *Am I making progress?*

If, in our effort to answer those questions, we use other people's fitness, food plans, or seeming serenity as standards for judging our recovery, we're headed for trouble. We'll end up trying to fix things that aren't broken. We'll switch to other people's food plans, eating schedules, or daily routines, even though our needs, life-styles, or biochemistry may be quite different from theirs. As a result, a relatively relaxed, more-than-adequate recovery can become a tense, nightmarish struggle.

You can learn how recovery works from other people but not how your recovery is progressing. That can be determined by you alone and only by comparing what you want from recovery with what you are getting. What works for you is the only reliable standard for judging any facet of your recovery program.

Generally speaking, when in doubt about your physical recovery, play it safe. If you're not sure about a food or activity, avoid it. Don't set weight goals. Try not to spend too much time alone. Reach out to people. Ask for help. Identify and talk about your feelings—and *take responsibility for your actions*. The most effective way to prevent a relapse is to own up to difficulties before they become disasters and let them teach you something about yourself, your disease, and your ongoing recovery.

Learn from Any Mistakes You Do Make

When we are aware of our old behavior patterns; the people, places, things, and thoughts that set them in motion; and the potential to relapse, we are capable of catching ourselves before we slip. But that doesn't mean we will. Everyone in recovery makes mistakes. Even the AA "Big Book" (AA World Services, Inc., 1976) notes that "no one among us has been able to maintain anything like perfect adherence to these principles." The goal in recovery is progress rather than perfection; the vital ingredient for success, a willingness to grow.

Consequently, if you should stray slightly off course or even take a major tumble back into compulsive eating, obsessive dieting, or bingeing and purging, make a conscious effort not to dump on yourself. Try not to conceal your missteps from others out of shame or fear of their disapproval. Eating disorders flourish in secrecy. Recovery occurs in the light. We experience more growth and progress by forgiving ourselves for our errors and figuring out what went wrong than by condemning ourselves as we've so often done in the past.

When you experience a setback, retrace the steps that led up to it. Ask yourself: *What have I done, seen, worried about, or heard in the past few hours, day, or days that might have set this off?* Perhaps the lovers you saw strolling in the park during your lunch hour stirred up memories of a relationship that didn't work out. Maybe you had a delayed reaction to the sarcastic remark you thought wasn't worth commenting on when your co-worker made it. Or you may have been fretting over an upcoming exam or business trip. Your slippery people, places, and things list can offer you clues. But you may not need them. Your answer often comes with the first thing that pops into your mind.

Although finding that answer doesn't change anything we've already done, it does teach us something new about ourselves, our disease, and the situations that seem to trigger cravings or precede slip-ups. Armed with this information, we can do the following:

1. *Put things into perspective.* Our mistake was not a blanket indictment of our worth as human beings or an indication that recovery is destined to fail the same way all the diets that came before it have. It was merely an act, one of thousands, both healthy and not so healthy, that will move us along in our recovery.

2. *Come up with alternatives* that will help us avoid making that same mistake again.

We can then give ourselves a sense of closure (and security) by making a written commitment to grow as a result of our past errors. Try the following format:

I am a good person even if I ___(mistake)___

Perhaps, in the future I can ___(alternatives)___

CHAPTER SEVEN

Welcoming Wellness:
How to Overcome Resistance and Start
Creating a New Life

I had been in relapse for six months when I realized that my inability to get back on track was not merely a matter of the wrong food plan, the wrong sponsor, or not trying hard enough. I *had* tried. And I had prayed . . . and soul-searched . . . and received mountains of advice that I dutifully followed for a day or two or several weeks. But each time I started to make progress, I barreled into the same brick wall.

I felt the same seemingly irresistible force pushing me back, warning me away, as if there were some unspeakable horror waiting for me around the next bend, something far more dangerous than any harm my eating disorder could cause me. I was astute enough to know that as long as I felt like that, I wasn't going anywhere. Yet, I couldn't seem *not* to feel it. I was stuck, paralyzed, frozen in my tracks by the implications of truly changing—*and by the prospect of operating in the real world without my dubious, but nonetheless familiar, shield of mood-altering foods and compulsive behavior.*

In the past, with fat as our problem, there was a clear-cut solution. We knew what we had to do and how to do it. The goal (lose weight) and the task (dieting) were familiar. Abstinence is not, and it creates a void in our lives. It takes away the mood-altering effects of food and compulsive behaviors and exposes us to emotions we've worked overtime to suppress. It eliminates the rituals and routines that once gave our lives a comforting predictability and shatters the illusion that the perfect diet will make us blissfully problem-free.

Many of us will miss the rush of excitement and optimism that used to accompany the start of each new "this is it, this time I'm really gonna do it" diet. We may not know what to do with ourselves once our days no longer revolve around eating or not eating. Worse yet, we're apt to become acutely aware of a gaping emptiness at the center of our being, a hole in our souls that we previously tried to fill with food.

Can we survive those losses? we may wonder. Or will we be overcome by emotion, abandoned by loved ones who don't like the ways we've changed? Couldn't we feel a hundred times more guilty, ashamed, worthless, and out of control than we ever felt after an eating binge—and have no way to make those feelings go away? Won't horrible truths about ourselves surface and destroy what little self-esteem we have left?

If we do manage to wade through the wreckage without falling apart completely, what will be waiting for us on the other side? Will we be better off than we were before or worse off than we ever imagined? Although we may not voice or even be fully aware of them, the vast majority of us are haunted by such questions. Our unconscious fear of what might happen once we stop using mood-altering substances or engaging in compulsive behavior can cause us to *resist recovery with every fiber of our being even though recovery is what we consciously want.*

Sticking with the Hell We Know

If you took physics in high school or college, you are apt to recall the first and third laws of motion: *an object tends to remain at rest or continue moving in the same direction unless it is affected by an external force;* and *for every force affecting it, an object exerts an equal and opposite force* (aimed at keeping or returning it to its original state). Well, the same principle can affect our physical recovery. A sort of psychological inertia can sap our strength, undermine our resolve, and increase the likelihood that we'll hang on to our old way of life even though it's no longer working for us.

It's as if there were a war going on within us. On one side is the part of ourselves that seeks recovery, even if only to escape the pain of our eating disorders. On the opposing side is the part of us that's determined to maintain the status quo at any cost. It equates change with disaster and loss. It is convinced that our survival depends on continuing to do what we've always done, and it uses every trick there is to persuade us that its point of view is true.

It is fairly obvious that this conflict is occurring when, from the outset or following a relapse, we find it virtually impossible to get or stay abstinent. We rationalize or blame external factors for our difficulty in much the same way we did while denying the existence or severity of our food addiction. There are other, more subtle telltale signs as well:

- Aches, pains, lingering colds, or stomach ailments. Our bodies almost always get into the act when our psyches are trying to stop us from changing.
- Using lots of "musts" and "shoulds" when referring to abstinence or other aspects of our recovery programs, making it sound as if we have no choice and no stake in our own recovery.
- Finding reasons to pay less attention to physical recovery.
- Deflecting positive input. This can range from wallowing in self-pity to taking compliments as veiled criticism of the way we used to be. "You look great" means "Boy, did you look awful before."
- Minimizing or completely negating our successes by reminding ourselves of how much further we have to go or telling ourselves that we'll probably blow it tomorrow. We're bracing ourselves for failure, probably believe that's what we deserve, and, more often than not, will unwittingly make sure that we get it.
- Setting up a failure support group. Rather than finding and sticking with "the winners," we get or remain close to folks who are skeptical about recovery programs or push food on us, assuring us that a little bit can't hurt.

In these and other ways, we subconsciously create conditions that can easily convince us to abandon our efforts to be abstinent. We will continue to do so until we're able to make the change-seeking part of ourselves strong enough to overcome the change-resisting part.

Overcoming Resistance by Welcoming Wellness

According to Abraham J. Twerski, M.D., author of *Self-Discovery in Recovery* (Hazelden Educational Materials, 1984), "A person will move from a situation he perceives as more detrimental and distressful to one he perceives as less so, but not the other way around." That is why, during early recovery, so much emphasis is placed on facing ugly truths about our food addiction and its chronic, progressive, potentially fatal nature.

Offering up nightmare images of the life we could return to counteracts our fear of change with a more powerful fear—that we could literally eat, diet, or binge and purge ourselves to death. There are limits to the effectiveness of fighting fear with fear, however. Change that is solely fear-induced can lead to fanaticism and has left many recovering individuals so full of dread that they actually wound up returning to their addiction for relief.

To forge ahead with courage and determination, we need more than the threat of relapse breathing down our necks. We also need something to look forward to, something to hope for, something to motivate us when even the prospect of being sick again can't convince us to keep going. That something is a clear, detailed picture of *physical, emotional, and spiritual wellness*, a mental blueprint for the full and fulfilling life we'll have a chance to build for ourselves *if we stay in recovery*.

Wellness is more than the absence of illness. It is a state of physical and psychological vitality and wholeness. With it, our lives are balanced and our outlook hopeful. We are of sound body, psyche, and soul. I and other recovering individuals have found it helpful to define and visualize that concept of future wellness in personal and concrete terms. Here's how.

❦

THE WELLNESS CIRCLE[*]

Take out a sheet of paper, the bigger the better, and on it draw a circle that practically fills the page. Divide your circle into twelve pie-shaped sections. Then add a small inner circle and a band around the perimeter to create a diagram that looks like this:

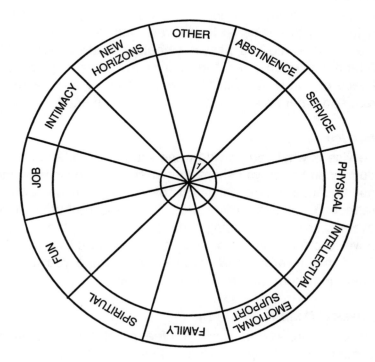

Label each section of the circle as I have. The labels represent the general components of wellness. After you read my

---

[*]This exercise is adapted with the author's permission from the Wellness Planning Board Strategy found in Dr. Sidney B. Simon's book *Getting Unstuck: Breaking Through Your Barriers to Change* (Warner, 1989).

brief descriptions of those components, think about what each one means to you personally. Ask yourself, "If my life were fulfilling in this area, who or what would be in it and what would I be doing?" As answers and images come to mind, jot down personal reminders in the appropriate section of the circle. Use words, phrases, abbreviations, even doodles. No one has to understand your notes but you.

Abstinence

Having said quite a bit about this topic already, I'll let you get right down to business. If you were well in this area of your life, what would you have? A healthy, realistic food plan? Attendance at one, two, three, or more OA meetings a week? Peace of mind? The ability to walk into your favorite restaurant and order an abstinent meal from the menu?

Service

Service is what you provide when you give to others unconditionally and when you share your strengths and skills willingly, not because you're obligated to or expect to be rewarded (although it's okay if you are). Service contributes to your overall sense of well-being because you believe that what you have to offer could be of value to someone else. To feel fulfilled in this area, how much service would you do? How often, for whom, where, and in what way?

Physical Health

Once you are well, how will you feel physically? What kind of condition will you be in? How will you maintain it? Where will exercise, stress reduction, or maintaining a healthy living environment fit into your overall life-style?

Intellectual Stimulation

Wellness involves a sound body and mind. You can exercise yours by exploring ideas that matter to you, looking into points of view that differ from your own, and learning in any way that suits you, from reading daily newspapers to taking continuing education courses or pursuing an advanced degree.

Emotional Support

Psychological fitness is part insight, part willingness to handle old situations in new ways, and a large measure of being backed up by other people. To be well, we need listeners and advisers, huggers and butt-kickers, friends of all kinds, and countless others. Who will these people be, and what will they offer you? In addition, when your life is fulfilling in this area, you won't isolate yourself. You will ask for help as needed. But how? And what else will you have or do?

Family

Your family is a group to which you permanently and unconditionally belong. In it you feel accepted as a person even on those occasions when your behavior is unacceptable. Consisting of people whom you love and accept in much the same way, it offers you the solid foundation of security to face life without addictive substances or activities. The family you picture as part of your well life-style need not be limited to, or even include, members of your immediate family or family of origin. Who will be in yours? What will you get from and give to them?

Spirituality

Under this heading falls anything related to your relationship with a Higher Power as well as anything you do to reach greater understanding of the realm outside your five senses. Fulfillment in this area might include prayer, meditation, organized religion, the practice of turning things over, and so on.

Fun/Humor/Excitement

Often overlooked and in short supply during early recovery, the things we do for sheer joy are an essential element of wellness. This includes behaviors children know as play and adults refer to as recreation—anything light, spontaneous, or downright silly.

Job/Career/Avocation

In other words, work, but not only for money or prestige. In fact, work that contributes to your sense of well-being is any undertaking, paid or unpaid, that enables you to feel productive or as if you are a valued participant in a team effort. What would be happening in this area of your life to bolster your overall wellness?

Intimate Relationship

By that I mean a close, loving connection to another human being, the give-and-take, trusting partnership that results when two people can be themselves while they're together and share their true thoughts and feelings with one another. Whether or not this is a basic human need continues to be debated, but most experts (and mothers) agree that there are few things as fulfilling as a healthy intimate relationship. What will yours be like when you are leading a healthy, happy life?

New Horizons to Explore

To stay physically, psychologically, and spiritually fit, we must continue to take on and master new challenges: see new places, meet new people, do things we've always dreamed we'd do. What risks would you take and which new horizons would you explore to enrich and fill up your life?

Other

This is a wild card. Make it anything you want or need to feel healthy.

After you've personalized all of the wellness components, think about each one's relative importance to you and give it a numerical ranking. Because abstinence needs to be your priority if you're going to have any shot at wellness at all, I've taken the liberty of giving it the number one rank for you. Number two would be the next most important, then three, four, and so on down to twelve—which would be the least important in comparison to the others. Write the number you're assigning each component in the appropriate section of the smaller inner circle.

❧

Even the Good Stuff Can Scare the Heck out of Us

Acknowledging our dreams is the first step toward realizing them, but many of us will find it surprisingly difficult to specify components of wellness, much less bring them into our lives. Indeed, merely thinking about a well future may stir up the same sorts of fear that imagining life without mood-altering foods and compulsive behaviors did.

Somehow it just doesn't feel safe or right to want what we want. Because years of food addiction and the circumstances that led up to it left us with a very low opinion of ourselves, we may not believe we deserve to be happy. We may have fallen short of that goal so many times that it seems foolish to expect better results in the future. *Don't get your hopes up,* we tell ourselves, *you probably won't succeed this time either.* And we're absolutely right. No matter how we try, *we can get only those things we believe we are capable and worthy of having.* Until we can *see* ourselves abstinent, physically fit, emotionally supported, and so on, our chances of being that way for more than a momentary fluke are indeed slim.

If we manage to beat the odds, we're apt to be skeptical. Since serenity and sobriety don't fit our internal picture of ourselves, we may feel guilty about our successes in recovery or become anxious when things are going well. *This can't last,* we tell ourselves, and in yet another well-intentioned effort to maintain the status quo, our psyches will make sure that our predictions come true.

Fortunately, we can change what we see in our mind's eye by planting positive, life-affirming images in it. We can give ourselves permission to dream and be happy and seek out whatever we need to live fully and meaningfully in recovery. In the process we can make the road ahead seem less perilous and keep ourselves more motivated to stay on it. So make advance reservations for a physically, psychologically, and spiritually full future.

Once you have an idea of what wellness means to you and what would go into a life you consider fulfilling, set aside some time over the next few days or weeks and practice picturing yourself with the life you want. You might get into a relaxed state and, taking one area at a time, visualize it in glorious detail, creating technicolor images of yourself already having the wellness you'd like in your future. You could write paragraphs or short essays describing each area as you imagine it will be one, two, or five years hence—and then reread and refine them. A list to which you can add new images periodically works well too. Or complete the following whimsical but nonetheless useful exercise.

❦

BACK TO THE FUTURE

Adopting a light, playful attitude, imagine that you've called ahead to reserve your future and will receive a letter confirming your reservation. Write that letter, using any voice you'd like—that of an enthusiastic cruise director, an impeccably organized hotel manager, or a reassuring, grandmotherly innkeeper. In the letter, detail all that will be waiting for you when you arrive at your destination.

You might word it like a publicity brochure: "Yes, you too will walk three exhilarating miles five glorious days per week! Then stop off at our well-stocked library and choose one book to read for sheer pleasure! Another to exercise your mind!"

Or try a tour guide format: "Serenity House is three miles

down Abstinence Road—which you'll be quite familiar with and comfortable traveling by now. It offers a wide range of spiritual growth opportunities. You'll be able to meditate daily, read brief inspirational passages, pray. . . ."

No matter how you do it, have fun with it. Assign it to the playful part of yourself that is naturally inclined to see the bright side of things. The result will pleasantly surprise you.

Hang on to what you've written and reread it regularly. Think about it when you feel your confidence sagging or your resistance building, and send yourself updates whenever new images of wellness come to mind.

❦

Visualizing your future in this manner differs from the magical thinking associated with your eating disorder. You are not conjuring up happily-ever-after pipe dreams and expecting them to be delivered gift-wrapped as a result of some unrelated event, such as getting thin or being abstinent. Instead, you are building a life for yourself one brick at a time with recovery as your cornerstone. You are bringing your dreams into clearer focus and using them, like lights at the end of a long, dark tunnel, to guide and encourage you to continue your journey.

What's more, you don't have to wait until you have weeks or months of abstinence to bring specific aspects of your vision of wellness to life. In fact, the sooner you get started the better. Working to bring something positive into your life—and not just to get rid of something negative—will enhance your overall recovery and make it easier to let go of old habits.

With your blueprint in hand, begin turning some of your dreams into realities right now. Pick one of the items you listed in your wellness wheel and state it as a goal. For example, "I will become more physically fit," or "I will do volunteer work that helps children," or "I will get involved in a relationship that could lead to marriage." Then figure out what achieving your goal will require you to

- *DO* (for example, join a fitness center and work out there at least three times a week or attend singles support group meetings)
- *GET* (for example, instructions on clowning from a course the YMCA is offering or a baby-sitter on the nights your support group meets)
- *BE* (for example, patient, or disciplined, or more open-minded about the men or women your friends arrange for you to meet)

Organize that information into a list of reasonable steps and start taking them one at a time. Count each step as a victory, and reward yourself for making progress. Make a list of rewards (nonedible, of course) and ways to celebrate your successes, if you think that might help, and claim your prize at each juncture along the road to your goals.

CHAPTER EIGHT

Supporting Physical Recovery
With Stress Management

"I was seeing an eating disorder counselor and going to group therapy for well over a year before I stayed abstinent for more than three or four days in a row," says Greg, a forty-five-year-old small-business owner. Greg is a compulsive eater whose weight reached an all-time-high of 375 pounds two years after his wife died, leaving him to raise two teenage boys on his own.

"I tried everything," he recalls. "Different food plans. Making pacts with other people in my therapy group. Joining OA. I met people there who were abstinent, and I could see that they were physically healthier than I was. They seemed more clearheaded and on top of things. I wanted what they had—I really did, but I just couldn't get it."

Sometimes it seemed as if he might. Greg would go along for several days following an abstinent food plan, telling himself that abstinence was his number one priority for that day and feeling hopeful. "But then something would happen at work or financially or with my kids, and it would throw me off completely," Greg says. During the year that he struggled to find abstinence, he weathered several major crises—most notably, his eighteen-year-old son's serious injury in a car accident and a threat by one of his best clients to take his business elsewhere.

"But the small stuff was just as bad," Greg claims. "I still had to give it my full attention, and it still made me tense and totally exhausted by the end of the day." That was when Greg's abstinence tended to fall by the wayside. On the way home from work, he'd decide that he was too tired to cook, so he'd stop at the supermarket, ostensibly to pick up something quick and easy—like a salad from the salad bar. The trouble was, he usually left with more than salad, including several of his favorite childhood comfort foods.

"Even if I stuck with the salad bar," he notes, "I'd include foods I'd agreed not to eat or pile up enough stuff to feed three people, and I'd eat it all. After all, I'd had a really rough day." Later, however, he'd be depressed or furious with himself for conning himself into overeating again.

Despite one false start after another, Greg didn't give up on recovery: "I heard people say, 'Keep coming back,' and I figured that even if I couldn't do anything else right, I could do that." After many months, it finally occurred to him that food wasn't the logical reward for making it through stressful situations and that maybe things would be less stressful if his eating disorder were in remission instead of making him angry at himself all the time. Ever since, staying abstinent has been easier for Greg.

"But I've got to be honest with you," Greg says. "I'm still tempted to give up my recovery whenever I'm under pressure or feeling overwhelmed and exhausted."

Most of us are. And many of us will give in to that temptation from time to time. Lasting recovery will remain just beyond our grasp because we keep falling into the same trap, *the stress trap*. We step into it each time we convince ourselves that the trauma of a major unexpected event or the accumulated pressure of daily demands is more than we can endure without some form of temporary escape or relief.

There is an element of truth to that perception, since all of us encounter situations that we can neither do anything to change nor accept as they are. Our only recourse is to flee—by physically removing ourselves from the situation or mentally tuning out our distressing thoughts and feelings.

For millions of men and women, having a drink or a doughnut, going to the racetrack or a shopping mall, or zoning out in front of the TV with a pint of Haagen-Dazs ice cream provides the momentary relief they require. But for those of us who are hooked on such substances or activities, the notion that they are useful for stress reduction is a dangerous one indeed.

The Stress Trap

Recovery is stressful because it asks us to make profound changes in ourselves without the benefit of the mood-altering substances and compulsive behaviors that used to cushion us. But it is made more so when, in addition to being compulsive eaters or bulimics, we're also stress junkies. And many of us are.

As active food addicts, we went to extremes not only in our eating or dieting practices, but in many other areas of our lives as well. That was extremely stressful. Many of us routinely overextended ourselves, taking on conflicting obligations and pushing ourselves to fulfill them until we were on the verge of collapsing. Then, when the stress in our lives exceeded our ability to tolerate it, we medicated ourselves with food.

If we maintain that same frenetic pace after we get into recovery and give up our "medication," we unwittingly set a stress trap for ourselves. We add what we need to do to be abstinent to the demands of our already jam-packed life-styles, feel overwhelmed a good deal of the time, and greatly miss the crutch on which we used to lean when we were about to crumble.

To further complicate matters, withdrawal from certain substances increases our sensitivity to normal stress, making it easy to mistakenly conclude that we're in intolerable, unchangeable situations and to overreact to them. At the slightest provocation, we're apt to tell ourselves that we're faced with a dilemma we can't put up with and don't know how to solve. And once we convince ourselves of that, our unmedicated minds start racing with worries about what might have gotten us into this jam and how we could have avoided it as well as the future catastrophes that might spring from it. Our stress level skyrockets, and with it, our desire for relief. Before we know it, we're questioning the value of remaining abstinent at all.

This isn't the right time, we think. *Sticking to a food plan is putting too much pressure on me, and I just can't take any more pressure right now.* Or we use Greg's rationale and tell ourselves that we're dealing with so much in so many areas of our lives that we're entitled to some peace and pleasure, that we've earned a night off from recovery and the right to pamper ourselves with comfort foods.

Before you fall for that faulty line of reasoning, stop and consider that the number one source of stress in any food addict's life is, always has been, and always will be food addiction. Consequently, a program of recovery is the best long-term stress management tool you'll ever find. In the short run, however, you'll need some additional alternatives to using mood-altering substances or compulsive behaviors for relief.

Here are a few you can put to good use right away. They'll not only help you keep stress at a tolerable level, but also prove to be lifesavers throughout your recovery.

- Relax
- Worry less
- Become a more effective decision-maker

Relax

In the past, we managed stress by *sedating* ourselves. We got keyed up and calmed ourselves with comfort foods. We exhausted ourselves but felt we couldn't stop to rest, and so instead we grabbed something sugary to boost our energy temporarily. When it wore off, we administered another dose. Then at day's end, we wound down with food and eating rituals, including sitting down to huge, heavy suppers and overloading ourselves with fats and starches that put us to sleep within an hour after mealtime.

These patterns and the foods we chose fogged our awareness, concealing our stressed, anxious, or depleted condition, but they did not change it. We went from overstimulated and overextended to *numb*, when the state we really needed was one of *relaxation*— measurably reduced physical tension and noticeably relieved mental pressure.

That sort of relaxation doesn't just happen, as you no doubt realized the last time someone urged you to "chill out" or "sleep on" a problem. In fact, the moment you attempt such measures, your mind is apt to zoom right in on the responsibilities or troubles that created the need to chill out in the first place. You wind up more anxious or exhausted rather than less so. More effective by far are various techniques that capitalize on the human mind's ability to alter bodily functions.

The first order of business is to relax physically, bringing yourself into what is sometimes referred to as an alpha state and bringing about changes in brain waves, pulse rate, respiration, and other bodily functions. There are a number of ways to do this, and alternatives to the method I'll be presenting can be found in books on stress management or visualization and guided imagery as well as on audiotapes that are available in most bookstores. All require five to fifteen minutes of uninterrupted time in a quiet location and a position that is reasonably comfortable for you. Sitting or reclining on a chair, sofa, or floor pillows is preferable to lying down. You want to relax, not fall asleep.

Slow down, center yourself, and release muscle tension. Once you're comfortably situated, shut your eyes and focus your full attention on your breathing. Take several long, slow breaths. Feel your diaphragm slowly rise as you inhale and gently fall as you exhale. Imagine that you are breathing out stress, tension, and worry while breathing in pure, cleansing, and relaxing white light.

Allow any other thoughts that pop into your mind to pass right through it, floating away as you return your focus to your breathing. Once it has taken on a calm, steady rhythm, switch your attention to your feet. *Tense* the muscles in your feet and *hold* the tensed position for a slow count of three. Then *release* and feel warm relaxation flow into the space where tension used to be.

Move your focus to your lower legs. *Tense* those muscles, *hold*, and after a slow count of three, *release*. Moving upward, train your attention on your thighs. *Tense-hold-release*, and enjoy the warm, heavy, relaxed feeling. At a leisurely pace, repeat this process for your buttocks, abdomen, and chest; your back, shoulders, and neck; your fingers, hands, arms, and facial muscles. Do this purposefully, always taking time to consciously experience the sensation of muscle relaxation and continuing to allow extraneous thoughts to simply wander through your awareness without commanding your attention.

Mentally scan your body for tightness, and use the tense-hold-release technique to relax the muscles in that area. When your body is completely relaxed, you'll feel a bit like a limp rag doll or as if you are floating.

From this relaxed state, there are several places you can go mentally. For your first few sessions, I recommend just floating, picturing a blue sky with clouds slowly passing by, or telling yourself how relaxed you are. Before opening your eyes and returning to the busyness of your life, plant some positive thoughts such as "This relaxed feeling will stay with me all day," or "I am reenergized, refreshed, and ready to tackle whatever lies ahead for me today."

Then take a mental vacation. One of the benefits of bringing ourselves into alpha state is the openness to new information and positive mental images it creates. We are able to let go of troublesome thoughts or worldly worries and travel to imaginary landscapes where we'll find solace, serenity, and even solutions to daily dilemmas that might never have occurred to us in our "normal" frame of mind. For pure relaxation, stress reduction, recentering and reenergizing, I suggest the following *Calm Scene.*

Once you've reached a physically relaxed state, take yourself on a mental journey to the most soothing, peaceful place you can imagine. You might choose a deserted beach, quiet cathedral, or clearing in the woods. You could picture yourself floating downstream in a canoe on a balmy afternoon, lying in a hammock under a starry sky on a cool spring evening, or wandering through a medieval castle that exists only in your mind's eye. You can select any locale your heart desires so long as your mind associates it with pleasure and calmness.

Put yourself in that place, and visualize every detail of it. Incorporate sights, sounds, scents, textures and other sensory information. Savor every nuance and the wonderful feeling of safety and serenity that this personal haven provides for you. Mark it in your mind, for this is the place you can go whenever you need a quick getaway from the pressures of real life. Each time you leave it, gently ease yourself away, saying good-bye and reminding yourself that you can come back.

Finally, take relaxation breaks whenever you need them. With practice, you'll be able to use relaxation techniques like the ones I've described to calm and center yourself anywhere, anytime, and in a matter of seconds. When you feel your stress level soaring or your energy dissipating, treat yourself to a quick trip to alpha state. It won't take any more time or ingenuity than your trips to the office candy machine or your in-home sneaky eating once did.

Just obtain some privacy—shut your office door, step into the nearest bathroom, go out to your parked car or around the next corner—and shut your eyes. Take several long, slow breaths and (1) imagine that you're exhaling tension and inhaling relaxation, (2) quickly picture yourself in your calm scene, or (3) tense-hold-relax muscles that tend to tighten up when you're under stress. You can even pursue option number three without removing yourself from the stressful situation. Simply focus on the muscles in your hands, feet, or other inconspicuous areas.

Worry Less

We can not only lower our stress level at will but raise it as well—and most of us do just that on a daily basis. We worry until we're overwrought and panic-stricken. Some of us confuse this with caring. We think we're demonstrating our concern about and commitment to important projects or relationships by worrying about them. Others among us are afraid *not* to worry. We believe worrying keeps us on our toes. We act as if going over and over the things we dread will somehow change the future and magically prevent our pessimistic predictions from coming true.

In reality, worry has no effect on external events and rarely inspires us to change. It merely makes us miserable, keeps us awake at night, hampers our concentration during the day, and poses an obstacle to taking positive action. So, begin to *identify your worrisome thoughts*. Anything beginning with "what if" generally falls under that heading, as do statements containing phrases such as "will ruin everything," "could really blow it," or "maybe I should/shouldn't have." Then *listen for them in your self-talk or conversations with others*. Each time they crop up, remind yourself that they are counterproductive and *dump them*. Actually imagine a giant trash can, and picture yourself depositing your worries into it.

Or *reframe* them, lowering your stress level simply by looking at people and events differently. A problem can be a catastrophe or an opportunity depending on your point of view, and the viewpoint you take is very much up to you.

Most of the time what's getting to us isn't what's actually happening but how we're perceiving it. We tell ourselves that we're in a do-or-die situation, that we can't handle certain circumstances, but it isn't true. *So say something else to yourself*, something that will help you feel more relaxed or confident. For more on this topic, see pages 169-172.

You can also *postpone* thinking about worrisome topics. Tell your worries, "Okay, okay, I hear you. Now go sit over there and be quiet. I'll get back to you later." Or try *setting a daily worry time*, and save up all your ruminating for that hour or so. But don't be surprised if that time arrives and you have little to stew over. More often than not, the matters you planned to get back to will have managed to work themselves out without your worrying about them.

Become a More Effective Decision-Maker
When it comes to decision making are you

- a *doormat*? Do you defer to other people's interests most, if not all, of the time?
- a *granite-chiseler*? Do you make up your mind easily enough but find it extremely difficult to change course once you do?
- a *procrastinator*? Do you postpone decisions until the last minute and then act on impulse only to regret—and eat over—it later?

- a *second-guesser?* Do you make yourself miserable by looking back on choices and wondering if you should have chosen something else?
- a *suggestion-collector?* Do you constantly ask for other people's advice but rarely use it and get so much of it that you're too confused to make a choice?
- a *rebel?* Do you make decisions based on the premise that whatever someone says you can't do is precisely what you will try to do?
- an *immediate gratifier?* Does your determination to have what you want when you want it often blot out all thoughts of future repercussions?

These are a few of the faulty decision-making processes that many of us once used. While they are problematic under any circumstances, when we carry them into recovery, they can sabotage our efforts to be abstinent as well as prevent us from taking full advantage of the new life we're being offered—and that's tragic. Instead, begin to

- generate alternatives
- analyze "costs" and "benefits"
- ask for help
- give yourself a grace period whenever possible.
- recognize that you can become a *more effective* decision-maker, but you'll never be a perfect one.

Generate alternatives. Although it may not always seem so at first glance, most circumstances that call for a choice to be made actually offer you plenty of alternatives from which to choose. Other people may be able to suggest some, and the situation itself may provide them if you do some investigating. The more factual information you have prior to making a decision, the better your chances of choosing what's best for all concerned.

Brainstorming, on your own or with others, is also a particularly effective (and fun) way to generate alternatives. First, clearly state the problem or describe the decision with which you are faced. Then come up with every conceivable solution or course of action. Be imaginative, playful, or downright weird if you want. The point is to get your creative juices flowing, so don't judge or discard any option during the brainstorming process. Just make as long a list as you can.

Analyze "costs" and "benefits." After your brainstorming list is complete, evaluate your options. Begin by eliminating those that are obviously out of the question. Next, from the items that remain, select *at least* three that seem reasonable to you. You can combine options if you'd like.

Then, consciously weigh the potential pluses and minuses of each. You may want to make a two-column chart for each alternative, listing the possible negative consequences in a costs column and the potential positive outcomes in a benefits column. To further clarify matters, you can give a numerical weight to each cost and benefit: a three (3) for very important, a two (2) for important, and a one (1) for relatively unimportant.

This process, which you can learn to do rapidly in your head, doesn't always reveal a clear-cut choice, but one option should begin to stand out. It may be the same option you would have instinctively chosen, in which case, you'll have your faith in your own good judgment restored.

In other instances, the cost/benefit analysis will shoot down your gut-level first choice completely. This is most likely to happen when you're attracted to a particular alternative because it could provide immediate gratification or help you avoid something you fear. It's usually in your best interest to exercise some impulse control or work through your fear (see pages 173-179) and go with the more logical choice.

The same holds true for high-cost/low-benefit options that still feel right. While your feelings are an important source of information, they change constantly and shouldn't be the sole basis for making any decision that is important to you.

On the other hand, if the cost/benefit analysis of your emotional choice comes out fairly close to the top-rated option, follow your gut instincts, especially if doing that will help you feel more comfortable with your choice.

Ask for help. While it's certainly beneficial to make more of your own choices, you don't have to make them entirely on your own. Other people can

- provide factual information
- offer options for your brainstorm lists
- listen to you voice your feelings and concerns
- help you see costs or benefits that you may have overlooked
- tell you what they chose to do under similar circumstances (and how they made their choice)

Just ask. But be careful about how and whom you ask. For example, if you're looking for someone to listen while you sort out your concerns or to help you see the broader picture, say that—and not "What do you think I should do?" Nine times out of ten, that question will net you practical advice that you aren't ready to hear and probably won't follow.

Likewise, seek out people who are capable of providing the kind of support you want. Finally, don't overdo. Polling everyone you know is a stalling technique, not a sound decision-making skill. All you get for your trouble is more conflicting information than you can possibly use.

Give yourself a grace period whenever possible. If after employing effective decision-making measures you still aren't certain about your choice and there's no hurry to act on it, try invoking the three-day rule. Identify the option you're leaning toward; then mentally set the entire matter aside for seventy-two hours. See how you feel about it when that grace period is up. Quite frequently, a more suitable solution will have come to mind, or you'll feel more willing to act on your earlier choice.

Recognize that you can become a more effective decision-maker, but you'll never be a perfect one. No one is. Despite our best efforts to make conscientious decisions, we'll sometimes make the wrong one. Sometimes we'll make the right one, but things will still go wrong. Will the world as we know it come to an end? Will our home, health, family, and future instantaneously be taken from us? Many of us act as if that were so and, in the process, increase our stress levels and our desire for a food fix.

An extraordinary fear of making mistakes is a trait that most compulsive eaters and bulimics share. We're terrified of doing the wrong thing at the wrong moment, ruining everything. This sense, irrational as it may be, that a single error can destroy a relationship or cost us our jobs can paralyze us with indecision and send us into a feeding frenzy.

When the prospect of choosing poorly horrifies us, we'll also put ourselves through untold misery each time the decisions we do make don't deliver the results we desire. We'll come down with cases of review neurosis and go over our experiences with magnifying glasses, looking for our fatal errors. *If only I'd done this instead,* we think. We berate ourselves for every perceived miscalculation. It's all a tremendous waste of energy.

Beating up on ourselves doesn't help us clarify anything or bring us peace of mind. So stop second-guessing and torturing yourself. Instead, ask yourself what you could do differently next time. *How can I use this situation to heal, grow, and enhance my recovery?* Turn your errors into opportunities to pick up some new information, develop new skills, cultivate new attitudes, gain personal insights, acknowledge your humanness—and maybe even have a good laugh. Then let go and go on.

PART III

EMOTIONAL, SOCIAL,
AND
SPIRITUAL RECOVERY

CHAPTER NINE

The Next Phase:
Emotional, Social, And
Spiritual Recovery

Abstinence is the foundation for recovery, but not the whole house. It's a path to wellness, a way to stop our downhill slide and free us from the grips of an illness that will physically, emotionally, and spiritually destroy us if left unchecked. We cannot have a healthier future without it. But eliminating addictive substances and compulsive behaviors won't automatically make our lives fulfilling.

Although we're unquestionably better off than we were when our lives revolved around eating, dieting, or bingeing and purging, we have not yet explored or accepted the parts of ourselves that our eating disorders concealed from us. We have not yet come face-to-face with whatever we were using mood-altering substances and activities to escape. As those issues and emotions start to catch up with us, our lives may seem less manageable rather than more so.

That is clearly the case for Lisa, a forty-four-year-old teacher and recovering compulsive eater. She has been abstinent for eleven months and plagued by anxiety attacks for the last three. "I've always been a worrier," she says, "but I've never *felt* like this before." Of course, she has always used something to numb herself before. Alcohol . . . or Valium . . . or cigarettes . . . or food. "Mostly food," Lisa acknowledges. She started eating compulsively early in her chaotic childhood.

Although no one realized it back then, Lisa's mother suffered from manic-depression, and her mood swings made home life completely unpredictable. "I never knew who I'd find when I got home from school, a madwoman or a depressed one," Lisa recalls. And that left her in a near-constant state of anxiety. By the age of nine, she was making daily stops at the corner store to purchase and occasionally shoplift candy bars. They somehow calmed her nerves. She also snacked from the moment she got home until bedtime. "It didn't matter what I ate," Lisa says. "As long as I was filling my stomach, I didn't feel it churning."

As an adult, Lisa found more to worry about and more ways to "treat" her anxiety. She says, "When things went wrong, I worried about them getting worse, and when they were going well, I worried about something coming along to ruin them." But she rarely felt the *emotional impact* of all that worrying. By reaching for drinks, smokes, tranquilizers, or chocolate, she kept her discomfort to a minimum.

Even during drug and alcohol rehab and through three years of sobriety, Lisa felt surprisingly little anxiety. "Of course, I gained eighty pounds and couldn't go for more than a few hours without eating something," she comments. Eventually, realizing that she was using food in the same way she had once used drugs and alcohol, she sought help from Overeater's Anonymous and, after months of slipping, became abstinent. But without food to tranquilize her, Lisa began to feel with full force a lifetime's worth of buried emotions.

"I'm okay if nothing's worrying me," she explains. "But if something is bothering me, I start feeling trapped and breathless and panicky. My hands shake, and my head throbs, and my heart beats so fast it feels as if it's going to fly right out of my chest. I want to run or hide under the covers on my bed." Or eat.

Each of Lisa's anxiety attacks is accompanied by what she describes as "an almost overpowering urge to stuff myself with any food I can get my hands on." And that makes her even more anxious. "I write and pray and make phone calls and eventually the food thoughts stop. But I'm terrified that at some point they won't, that one day the anxiety will be so overwhelming that I'll say 'To hell with abstinence' and dive right back into the food."

Lisa's fear is quite likely to be realized. Both her happiness and her abstinence are being jeopardized by the very same feelings and beliefs that led to and perpetuated her food addiction.

As Lisa has discovered, recovery begins with abstinence but does not end there. While actively involved in our eating disorders, we walked around in a fog. In recovery, without foods to alter our moods or obsessions about dieting and weight to divert our attention, that fog lifts, offering us a new outlook on life. But abstinence also reveals problems that early recovery practices alone cannot resolve.

Soon after we start abstaining from compulsive eating or bingeing and purging, we begin to catch glimpses of various realities that our eating disorders had been concealing from us. We may experience fear, anxiety, sadness, or anger that is more intense than our immediate circumstances seem to warrant or spontaneously recall painful or shameful incidents from our past.

The realizations we'll come to—that our childhoods might not have been quite as happy as we'd convinced ourselves they were or that we were rarely as "fine" as we claimed to be—will be no more pleasant to face than the facts about our eating disorders were. But face them we must. Until we do, we can't write our own script for the future, and worse yet, we are virtually doomed to repeat our mistakes and suffer the same unhealthy consequences.

What We're Asked to Do in Phase Two

Although we cannot change our past, we can learn from it and do things differently in the future. In the second phase of recovery, our goals are to

- fearlessly seek out truths about our lives and share our findings with at least one other person—a friend, priest or rabbi, OA sponsor, support group, or therapist
- thoroughly examine and feel the impact of the unresolved issues we uncover

- recognize that we have options today that we may not have had when trying or traumatic experiences originally occurred and become willing to explore those options

In this phase, we let go of the excess baggage we've been carrying for years and start to repair old relationships as well as develop healthy new ones. In a process of self-renewal that is sometimes bitter, sometimes sweet, always challenging, and ultimately liberating, we heal old wounds.

We free ourselves from the guilt and shame associated with past experiences, forgive ourselves for the things we did to ourselves and other people while we were caught up in our food addiction, and eventually find that staying abstinent has become less of a struggle for us. As Kara, the date rape survivor, puts it, "When I was able to face my demons in therapy and handle the pain without stuffing myself, it finally occurred to me that maybe I didn't really need the food to cope after all."

Because each of us has different issues and priorities, the tasks associated with emotional, social, and spiritual recovery are not quite as clear-cut and universally applicable as earlier ones. What's more, since insight is infinite and relationships are multilayered and ever-changing, we may be dealing with certain issues for the rest of our lives.

If you are like most compulsive eaters and bulimics, this thought is not encouraging. You are probably thinking that everything you've just read makes up an impossibly tall—and disquieting—order. "Is it really necessary to dredge up the past?" you may ask. "Do I really need to go poking around in my psyche, looking for trouble and maybe stirring up so much of it that I'll get back into the food? And won't it be painful? Humiliating? Couldn't I just follow my food plan and work my recovery program the way I have been?"

Yes, you could. If you're worried about what you might find during this phase of your recovery, you can refuse to look. But you'll be taking a big risk. While we don't have to resolve all of our internal and interpersonal conflicts to overcome eating disorders, ignoring them all is at best a barrier to leading a full life and often an invitation to relapse.

If we do remain abstinent, we're apt to reach for something else (cigarettes, sex, work) to make us feel better when we're feeling bad. We may become obsessed with something other than eating and our weight (our marriages, our children, our recovery program) and focus our attention on that concern to the exclusion of all else. And we'll eventually develop the same destructive relationship with those substances or activities that we once had with food. We can't help it. We still have an addict's mentality that knows how to get to only one destination—addiction and despair.

We are like houses built on crumbling foundations. No matter how thoroughly we remodel the buildings, unless we repair the underlying structures, our new, improved dwellings won't stand for long. To truly overcome our eating disorders and develop a lasting sense of physical, emotional, and spiritual well-being, we need to patch the cracked cinder blocks, replace the rotting beams, and construct a new foundation that supports our new way of life. We must do the following:

- *Uncover the impact of and complete unfinished business.* Look for any event or experiences from the past that still stir up strong emotions when we think about them and/or trigger an urge to act out when we encounter similar situations.

- *Identify and work through unresolved issues.* Focus on any conflicts, concerns, or problems that periodically or continually reappear in our lives, creating anxiety, confusion, or other obstacles to wellness. Control, trust, acknowledging or expressing feelings, neglecting our own needs, all-or-nothing thinking, low self-esteem, fear of abandonment, and difficulty giving or receiving love are a few of the issues that plague compulsive overeaters or bulimics.

- *Become aware, challenge, and revise faulty psychological programming* we've been carrying around since childhood. Write out some of the beliefs about yourself and other people and how to handle upsetting situations that adversely affected your self-esteem and directly or indirectly set off bouts of compulsive behavior.

- *Find new ways of thinking, acting, and relating to people* that will enhance our self-esteem instead of damaging it and improve the quality of our lives rather than diminishing it.

Accomplishing these tasks will not be easy or painless. The road to self-discovery, self-acceptance, and emotional, social, and spiritual recovery can be bumpy. Traveling it requires

- Courage
- Patience
- A supportive and forgiving attitude toward yourself

Courage

Delving into our backgrounds for the reasons behind our eating disorders is frightening. We fear that we'll be overwhelmed by emotions or destroyed by the truths we discover. That fear will be quite intense at times, but always more intense than anything we actually encounter.

Recalling events from earlier in our lives does not mean reliving them as the helpless children, confused adolescents, or humiliated younger adults we once were. While certain memories can stir up unsettling emotions, they are still only memories or, as a therapist friend of mine puts it, scary movies with fake blood and special effects. We limit the power our fears wield over us by reminding ourselves that, as terrifying as they may seem while they're on our mental movie screens, imaginary monsters can't reach out and strangle us.

What's more, we own the movie theater. We can choose what we look at, when, and in how much depth. If memories or insights become too painful, we can turn off the projector, switch films, and watch something else for a while. There are plenty of areas to explore, and all of them are best dealt with in small, manageable doses.

Patience

The process takes as long as it takes. As you get closer to completing this phase of recovery, it will become easier for you to think and talk about certain subjects. They will have less of an emotional impact on you and less influence over your behavior. You'll begin to see that you are more than what your past experiences led you to believe and that there are more effective ways to live. You'll realize that your old ways of coping with people and problems can never heal you.

When you reach that point, you'll be able to let go of your old grievances. You won't forget the past or deny it or tell yourself it didn't matter. But you will relinquish your emotional attachment to it. You'll stop looking back to blame or think about the life you might have led if only you, your parents, or your circumstances had been different. Instead, you'll look ahead, develop new attitudes and skills, and from that day forward, take responsibility for your own actions.

However, you spent a long time sliding downhill, and although it won't take you as long to climb back up, you aren't going to heal overnight. You're in the process of becoming a new person, of reentering the real world with a whole new set of attitudes and behaviors. That process can't be hurried or expected to proceed from start to finish without a few upsets. There will be times of grief, doubt, and discouragement, times when you question the value of what you're doing, and times when your life seems to be staying the same or getting worse, despite your best efforts.

If your boss still treats you like dirt, or your spouse still seems more interested in work than in you, or every person you've dated has resembled an escapee from a chain gang, you're bound to wonder whether working so hard on recovery is worth the effort. "What's the point?" you'll ask. "Life still stinks. Maybe living for my next binge or weigh-in is all I'm entitled to and the best I'll ever be able to do." To avoid this pitfall, do the following:

- Make sure you are in recovery for your own sake and not to change somebody else. Commit yourself to do whatever is necessary for you to be healthy, serene, and fulfilled.

- Further develop your faith in a Higher Power. As you did in phase one, allow yourself to draw strength from a force greater than your own ego. Ask for guidance and protection. Your Higher Power will see to it that you don't get more than you can handle. If you're not sure you believe that, act as if you do.

- Focus on the process, not the outcome. Look at what you need now and what you are doing to meet those needs now rather than worrying about and trying to control what happens a day, a week, or a year from now.

- Reduce stress in other areas of your life during particularly difficult transitions. For example, while I was working through some of my more painful issues in therapy, I needed to devote more emotional energy to taking care of myself and less to taking care of other people. So I stopped sponsoring OA newcomers for a while. You may need to cut back too or to work less overtime, declare a temporary moratorium on looking for Ms. or Mr. Right, or put some distance between yourself and certain family members.

A Supportive and Forgiving Attitude Toward Yourself

It's impossible not to regret some of the things we did or failed to do in the past, and it is all too easy to become merciless self-critics at this point in our recovery. However, all we get from beating ourselves up over our past is additional—and unnecessary—pain. The misery our eating disorders have already caused us is payment enough for having them.

There's no value in bombarding ourselves with "should haves" and "could haves." The guilt and shame induced by such thinking were driving forces behind our addictive behavior, and they can pose a serious threat to abstinence and recovery. Subconsciously punishing ourselves for our past crimes, we may abandon both, declaring ourselves hopeless. Here are some actions you can take to reduce the likelihood that you'll engage in this form of self-sabotage:

Begin immediately to approach yourself with dignity and respect.

Acknowledge who you are: a multidimensional, lovable, capable human being recovering from a cunning and powerful chronic illness that you did not intentionally acquire and which you will not keep in remission by treating yourself like a criminal. Be kind. Compassionate. Patient and encouraging. Give yourself credit for your accomplishments. Talk to yourself as you would a cherished friend. In fact, make a vow to stop saying anything to yourself that you wouldn't say to someone whose friendship you hope to keep.

Try to forgive yourself for your past. Regardless of the outcome, you were doing the best you could at any given moment with the knowledge, skills, and support that were available to you. If you could have done better, you would have. What's more, you're doing a good many things better already.

Remind yourself of past accomplishments as well as the progress you've made since beginning recovery. And move as quickly as possible from identifying your errors in judgment or behavior to developing alternatives for handling similar situations in the future.

Spend more time with nourishing people and in places where your needs are met in healthy ways. Cultivate friendships for fun, intellectual stimulation, outdoor adventures, and group activities, as well as for emotional support and recovery-related pursuits. Take classes and walks in the woods. Go to libraries and museums and on vacations that fill you up with wonder and relaxation instead of excess food and liquor.

Take care of yourself physically. Get enough rest. Make sure that you are meeting the dietary requirements for your age group, gender, or special needs. If necessary, take vitamin or mineral supplements. Exercise often and intensely enough for cardiovascular fitness and to receive the benefits of increased endorphin production. These natural painkillers create a sense of well-being that you'll eventually welcome, even if you start out hating every step of your thirty-minute walk.

But don't overdo. As many a recovering bulimic or anorexic can tell you, exercise can be addicting. If you're not an athlete and you exercise for more than one hour a day or feel you *have* to, no matter how tired you are, you're going overboard and could be developing a dependency on your workout.

Get Support

Although the inner voice of super-self-sufficiency may be saying, "I should be able to do this myself," you'll get farther faster when you work through old material with outside assistance

Discussing these matters with supportive friends or fellow eating disorder sufferers will be enough for some of us. But many of us have such complicated, longstanding, and painful concerns to work through that we'll require the assistance of a knowledgeable helping professional. If that's the case for you, then therapy is definitely an option worth considering. I encourage you to set aside any reservations you may have and wholeheartedly pursue it.

The Willingness to Feel, Heal, and Change Your Behavior

This, according to author Sharon Wegscheider-Cruse, is the key to lasting recovery, and I couldn't agree more. While insight is an important foundation for change, it alone changes nothing. If we want different results—more self-esteem, better relationships, healthier life-styles—we must live more consciously and behave differently.

The deeper we get into this stage of recovery, the more apparent it becomes that we could work on ourselves forever and never really be done. Below each layer of faulty thinking and unfinished business lies another layer, and another. Trying to uncover and completely resolve them all can turn us into perennial navel-gazers. We could stay so busy *improving* ourselves that we'd never get around to *being* ourselves. Make sure you are learning about yourself to enhance your life and not working on yourself to avoid living your life.

Telling ourselves that we aren't ready to date because we're still working on intimacy issues or that we'll ask for the raise we deserve after we finish dealing with our feelings about authority figures is a trap. We're treating our lives as if they were dress rehearsals. The purpose of emotional, social, and spiritual recovery is to help us get on with the show. So find out what you need to know, and use that information to do what you need to do. Don't wait until your internal changes are completed before beginning to make external ones.

This is of the utmost importance where our physical recovery is concerned. Although we can begin the tasks of this recovery stage before we become abstinent or continue them if we should lose our abstinence, we cannot actually accomplish them while we are still numbing and distracting ourselves with food and compulsive behavior.

CHAPTER TEN

Four Basic Tools for Recovery

As difficult as it may be for those of us with eating disorders to believe, many people *take it for granted that life has its ups and downs*. They actually *accept* that some days will be better than others, that sometimes they'll feel miserable and they'll be able to do nothing about it. They aren't thrilled about that state of affairs, and their immediate reaction may be to pour themselves a stiff drink, dig into something sweet, or otherwise attempt to alter their mood artificially. However, because they also have *confidence in their own coping skills as well as prior experience handling various dilemmas of everyday living*, they quickly get themselves back on track. They look for the things they *can* change, get busy doing just that, and bounce back.

Both before and after entering recovery, most of us compulsive eaters and bulimics looked at such individuals with awe and envy. They seemed so healthy, so sure of themselves, so . . . lucky, as if they had been blessed with a secret formula for living well and fully that we could never hope to have. This was a misconception on our parts, for there is no foolproof formula bestowed on some and withheld from others.

Men and women who appear to naturally take what each day gives them and make the most of it weren't born with that ability. They *developed* it—and generally had more opportunities to do so than we did. While we were busy eating, dieting, purging, or worrying about our weight, they were learning confidence-building, relationship-strengthening skills and attitudes *that we can learn, practice, and adopt too*. The only difference is that we have to do that now, as clean, sober, abstinent adults, rather than as relatively unscathed youngsters. We must simultaneously learn and unlearn, and while that may not always be easy or fun, it can be done—and considering the potential benefits, it is worth doing.

In this chapter and the two that follow it, you'll find self-help strategies addressing the very issues we compulsive eaters and bulimics need to resolve. None are the ultimate solutions for any problem area or substitutes for the things you know you must do to overcome your primary problem—an addiction to mood-altering substances and activities. They simply offer you a number of specific alternatives for effectively dealing with many of the feelings and conflicts that used to trigger your obsessions and compulsions. I invite you to locate the sections that correspond to your concerns and take advantage of the advice you find there.

Reacquaint Yourself with Yourself

Although many of the attitudes, habits, and problems that have kept our obsessions and compulsions alive are the result of how we were treated, we also created our own problems while living from food fix to food fix or diet to diet.

As our urge to eat compulsively, diet obsessively, or binge and purge became more powerful and time-consuming, we may have developed personality traits that wreaked havoc in our lives: impatience, sarcasm, procrastination, dishonesty, and a tendency to isolate ourselves; chronic guilt, shame, and self-contempt that we naturally tried to squelch with addictive behavior. We also may have let our careers, relationships, social lives, and other things go unattended and, as a result, found ourselves in new crisis situations that we coped with in the same old, addictive way. The more we did that, the more estranged from ourselves we became. We disowned both our strengths and our limitations, downplaying or entertaining grandiose fantasies about the former and working feverishly to conceal or compensate for the latter.

Having lost ourselves under layers of fat, mountains of food, and a seemingly endless stream of obsessions and compulsions, we must find ourselves again once we are in recovery. We must get to know who we are—warts and all—because the self-acceptance and self-esteem we'll need to maintain and benefit from our new way of life cannot be achieved without self-knowledge.

When we peer below the surface of our lives, we are apt to see many less than admirable traits. If we are only digging up our misdeeds, we will end up horribly depressed. That is why, while taking stock of ourselves and our lives, we'll want to *look at the pluses as well as the minuses*—the things we did well; the goals we accomplished; the kindnesses we showed others; the strengths, survival skills, and compassion we developed; the errors we've already corrected; the growth we've already experienced; and other positive aspects of our personalities.

If you are in a Twelve Step program, you can take stock by completing a Fourth Step inventory and working Steps Five through Nine. A sponsor, AA's *Twelve Steps and Twelve Traditions* or *The Twelve Steps of Overeaters Anonymous*, and other recovery literature may prove helpful. If you are not in a Twelve Step program or simply want to check in with yourself, try drawing a two-column chart in your recovery journal, labeling one column with a plus sign (+) and the other with a minus sign (-) and listing your positive and negative traits in the appropriate columns. Include skills, abilities, shortcomings, habits, attitudes, achievements, failures, the way you treat yourself and other people, how you've lived up to your values, and any other attributes or drawbacks you can think of.

If the list in your minus column is significantly longer than the one in your plus column, you're probably being too hard on yourself. Eliminate negatives that you've already taken steps to remedy. Or lengthen your positive list by adding some of the things you've learned because of some of your negatives; this could include making an extra effort to talk to people because of your shyness or, because of your difficulty accepting compliments, smiling and thanking people when they say something nice about you.

When your list is complete, find someone you trust and share it with him or her. That person will be able to help you put some of your negatives into perspective or add more positives to your list.

Then write encouraging statements for each item on both lists. For your pluses, try, "I am proud of *(positive attribute)* and plan to build on this strength in the future." For your minuses: "I accept all of who I am including *(negative attribute)*. If I could have done better I would have—and in the future I will."

Finally, take steps to alter any character defects that may be undermining your relationships, recovery, or ability to accept yourself. Try the following:

- Identify behaviors that arise from specific weaknesses that you listed in your personal inventory. For example, because you tend to be overly critical of others (an item on your minus list), their flaws may be the first thing you notice and you may rarely miss an opportunity to point out their mistakes.

- Come up with an opposite or alternate behavior. For instance, try to spot something positive about others within the first twenty seconds of any interaction and, where appropriate, pay a compliment.

- Test out your alternatives and pay attention to the results. If you aren't happy with them, you can always try something else. If you are happy with the results, keep practicing your new behavior. It soon will become a positive habit—and a source of positive self-esteem.

Rethink

We used to think the worst. Given the chance, we could find a cloud for every silver lining, a flaw in every plan, an accident waiting to happen around every bend. We predicted failure, expected rejection, and ran ourselves ragged trying to prevent disasters or prepare ourselves for the "inevitable" instead of concentrating on what we did want and how best to get it.

We magnified and personalized. Unpleasant events were "horrendous," "devastating," or "catastrophic." Entire days were "ruined" by minor incidents that disappointed us. Nights of sleep and weeks of serenity were lost to conjuring up worst-case scenarios and then scaring ourselves silly worrying that they would come true.

This distorted thinking was an integral part of our eating disorders. Our assumptions and premature conclusions instigated the moods we felt compelled to alter through compulsive eating, frantic dieting, or bingeing and purging. Then we condemned ourselves for what we'd done, triggering the guilt, shame, and need for calming or control that kept our addictive cycle going.

Because they are deeply ingrained habits, all of us brought our self-defeating thought patterns with us into recovery—and frequently found them turning our lives into waking nightmares. Thanks to our faulty perceptions, mild nervousness mushroomed into full-blown panic attacks, minor disappointments led to major depressions, or tiny slips in physical abstinence unleashed a barrage of self-condemnation that sent us plummeting into prolonged relapses.

What we can do instead is recognize that our thoughts are only *ideas*, not realities. Our perceptions are not necessarily accurate, reasonable, or the *only* way to view our circumstances. We can discard self-defeating thought patterns and replace them with new mental habits that increase feelings of competence, confidence, and courage as well as improve our chances of leading full and fulfilling lives.

Start by paying attention to your current thought patterns, especially when you're feeling upset. Step back and examine your self-talk. What are you telling yourself about yourself, other people, or the situation you've encountered? Are you drawing comparisons to past experiences that turned out poorly? Are you predicting future problems? Putting yourself down? Using phrases such as "Why does this always happen to me?" "I'm entitled," "Serves me right," or variations on other messages? Also watch out for *shoulds, awfuls, terribles, musts, can'ts, nevers,* and *if onlys.*

Then examine the validity of your perceptions. Just because you think something is so doesn't make it so. Our beliefs are not facts. Indeed, the gap between our experiences and our interpretation of those experiences can be enormous. So watch out for misperceptions. Are you sure that waitress is intentionally ignoring you or that your boss's delay in responding to your memo is proof that he or she has it in for you? Couldn't there be another explanation? Perhaps the waitress has a headache or is confused about the tables in her station. Maybe your boss is waiting to hear from his or her boss or has misplaced your memo.

Your best bet is to cut out the "color commentary" altogether and stick with the facts. The waitress has not been to your table. Your boss has not responded to your memo. What do you want to *do* about that? Less tangible data—someone's motives, expectations, or reaction to you, for example—is not needed as often as you may think, and it's often impossible to obtain. Guesswork in this area generally does more harm than good. The meanings we attribute to other people's words and actions are notoriously inaccurate. So check out your assumptions when you can. And when you can't?

If you don't like your original interpretation, try a different one. In fact, before you draw any conclusions, especially in emotionally charged situations, come up with a minimum of three possible explanations for what you've encountered. Make sure that at least one would create a different feeling and bring about a more positive outcome than your initial reaction would.

Then act as if the more advantageous interpretation is accurate. Behave as you would if you truly believed that waitress had a headache or your boss misplaced your memo. See what happens. I'll bet you'll be pleasantly surprised.

Change the way you word your self-talk. Don't use such strong language. Instead of thinking, "*I can't stand it* when . . . ," try "*I don't like it* when . . ." Replace "This is *killing* me" with "This is *hurting* (or *putting pressure*) on me."

Stay away from absolutes. Replace *always* with *sometimes* or "This *always* happens to me" with "This has happened to me before." For even greater impact, you might add, "so I know I can survive it" or "I've learned how to deal with it." Stop telling yourself that your "*entire day is ruined*" or that you *never* get what you want. Instead, file a factual report: "Something just happened that I hadn't planned on, and I'm upset about it right now," or "I'm disappointed that I couldn't get what I wanted in this particular situation."

Learn more about "rethinking," and practice, practice, practice.
You really *can* control and change the way you think and, in turn,
the way you feel and behave. Indeed, one highly effective form of
short-term psychotherapy—cognitive therapy—is based on that
principle and is thoroughly described by David Burns in *Feeling
Good: The New Mood Therapy* (Wm. Morrow, 1980). A multitude
of rethinking strategies can be found in that book and others that
appear in the suggested reading list at the end of this book.

Reprogram

"Garbage in, garbage out," people in the computer field like to say,
referring to the fact that computers can only perform the functions for which they were programmed and process only the data
made available to them. If the input they receive is inadequate,
inaccurate, or not applicable to the task at hand, their output will
be too. The same can be said for us humans—the majority of
us have been operating for most of our lives with self-limiting
programming.

"You can't trust anyone," we tell ourselves.

"You better have a career, 'cause you'll never nab a husband."

"You're weak-willed . . . gluttonous . . . lazy . . . ungrateful. . . ."

Messages such as these, which we originally received during our
formative years, have become personal credos that we *recite to ourselves* daily, sometimes hourly. These and similar messages tend to

- stir up tremendous anxiety, or even self-hatred, which we try to
  bury under a mountain of food or fix by dieting or purging
- turn into self-fulfilling prophecies that undermine our
  achievements
- instill in us a pervasive sense of helplessness and futility that
  perpetuates our eating disorders and can undermine recovery

What we can do instead is *reprogram* ourselves, replacing our pessimistic and self-defeating beliefs with more accurate and optimistic
ones that enhance our self-esteem. We can feed our brains data
that is a closer, more validating reflection of who we are and who

we hope to become. As a result, our chances for success and fulfillment at any endeavor—including recovery—increase dramatically.

Say It's So

The following positively worded statements are called affirmations, and they are an excellent tool for reprogramming our psyches:

... I am serene and relaxed.
... I intuitively know how to handle work-related situations.
... My mind is clear and receptive to new ideas.
... I am lovable, capable, and recovering.
... I am in fit physical, emotional, and spiritual condition.

Affirmations create soothing, confidence-building mental pictures that can be woven into our mind-sets in the same way our negative beliefs were—through repetition.

Affirmations are simple and direct: "I accomplish what I set out to do," rather than "When I put my mind to it, I'm usually able to accomplish something every day."

They are positively worded: "I have the courage to go out and meet new people," rather than "I'm not afraid to go out and meet new people."

Affirmations usually refer to future events or conditions in the present tense: "I am a recovering food addict with long-term abstinence," rather than "I am going to be . . . ," "I can be . . . ," or "I will be a recovering food addict with long-term abstinence." Although the latter may appear closer to the truth—especially if more than two or three days of back-to-back abstinence continues to elude you—saying that you already have what you want makes a more powerful impact on your psyche and your behavior. You will be more inclined to make choices and take actions consistent with *being* a recovering food addict with long-term abstinence. These actions and choices are different from those of someone who will be a recovering food addict someday but is not one yet.

Say It Again and Again

During every waking moment, we talk to ourselves. Even when we aren't consciously attending to the messages we send ourselves, those ideas, images, evaluations, and interpretations are getting through to us—and directly or indirectly influencing everything we do.

Our self-talk creates a path of least resistance, a groove we gravitate to time and again, like rainwater running downhill in the same course that zillions of raindrops have taken before. The only way the rain will change course is if something, a rock slide, let's say, changes the terrain, creating a new path of least resistance.

The same holds true for you and me. But we don't have to wait for a rock slide. We can create new paths of least resistance, leading to new destinations of our own choosing, through the conscious repetition of new self-talk.

⚜

SELF-TALK EXERCISE

Write some self-talk of your own—brief, to-the-point affirmations like the examples I've already given or clusters of compatible ideas like the following:

- "I like how I feel and how I think. I like how I look and how I do things. I approve of myself and am proud of the person I've become."
- "I am hopeful and healthy and full of life. I'm glad to be alive. I'm glad to be growing and learning and taking positive risks. So many good things are coming to me now that I'm embracing life."

After you've come up with a dozen or so affirmations and other forms of positive self-talk, read your writings out loud *with feeling*. Recite these motivating and validating statements about yourself forcefully and with confidence. Repeat each a minimum of three times.

If you like, record your affirmations on an audiocassette.

Go through the entire sequence of affirmations and self-talk three times, and on either the second or third repetition, change the pronoun from "I" to "you." Addressing yourself in that manner reinforces the message.

Listen to your tape or recite your positive self-talk at least once a day. Try it first thing in the morning, while driving or riding in a car, or when you're exercising or taking a walk or right before bed.

Affirmations take root particularly well if you plant them when you're in alpha state. So take the time to run a few through your mind each time you relax or meditate. You might even make a personal reprogramming tape that includes instructions for getting relaxed, followed by a bit of soothing music to imagine calm scenes by, and then a few minutes worth of positive self-talk.

⚜

Write

We used to keep our emotions bottled up inside us and allow our concerns to·run in circles through our minds. Because we didn't bring them out into the light of day for closer, more objective inspection, the fear and confusion surrounding them often grew to monstrous proportions—which we coped with in our same old addictive way.

As we began our recoveries, we started to share our worries and wishes with our sponsors or therapists and fellow compulsive eaters and bulimics. We soon learned that talking about the things that bothered us lightened the load we'd been carrying (and eating over) and gave us an opportunity to gain a more realistic, useful perspective on our problems.

Regrettably, supportive people are not always available when we need them. Sometimes, especially during early recovery, we'll have trouble trusting others enough to share what is really going on inside us. Banishing our feelings and concerns to the pit of our stomach or back of our mind is not a healthy alternative. Fortunately, there is another—*writing* about our problems, hopes, fears, resentments, and so on. By carrying on conversations on paper, we'll often learn as much as we would by talking to someone else—and sometimes more.

Make "Where I'm at This Very Minute" Journal Entries

A recent telephone conversation has left you bewildered, and an unidentified feeling, possibly one that you used to mislabel "hunger," is washing over you. Even if you could call a support person, you wouldn't know what to tell him or her—because you don't really know what's going on inside you. Now's the time to pull out your journal or a few sheets of paper and try some stream-of-consciousness writing.

Start simply. Jot down a few factual observations: "I am sitting at the kitchen table. I can smell the coffee brewing and hear my neighbor's telephone ringing. . . ."

Keep writing anything that pops into your mind, and you'll soon discover that you've moved on to something significant: ". . . neighbor's telephone ringing. I hope mine doesn't, because it will probably be Marge and she'll probably want to tell me how awful her life is—*again*. It really ticks me off that she never listens when I'm upset. . . ."

When you feel finished, reread what you've written, and pay particular attention to anything that seems to grab you. You may find the issue behind your unsettled state, some possibilities for dealing with it, other insights about yourself, or bits of faulty thinking that can be corrected immediately. Almost always, you'll feel better and be able to get on with your day.

Write "Dear Higher Power" Letters

Whether you think of the power greater than your own ego as God, a group of people, or a wise, spiritually oriented part of yourself, you can pour out your sorrows or joys, confusions or desires, to that source of strength and comfort. With the tone and honesty you'd use to address a friend or confidant whom you trust completely, write letters to your Higher Power. Tell of your current situation. Recap the pluses as well as the minuses. Ask for the guidance you need. More often than not, you'll find it coming through to you in the words that flow freely from your pen.

Write Dialogues

Compose conversations between yourself and your Higher Power; yourself and a specific emotion; or yourself and the child, parent, critic, addict, cheerleader, or wise adviser within you. Ask your dialogue partner questions. Respond to the answers. Probe, disagree, correct misperceptions, or request solutions. The variations—and insights you'll gain—are endless. (For an example of this process, see pages 175-176.)

Write and Release

This technique, which can be done daily or as needed, involves

- noting on a slip of paper the things over which you feel powerless
- declaring in writing that you let go of your emotional attachment to that matter and turn it over to the care of a power greater than yourself
- depositing the slips of paper in a jar, coffee can, or shoe box set aside expressly for that purpose

This small, positive ritual has served as an effective alternative to worry and the need to overcontrol for many, many recovering individuals. It cements our commitment to accept the things we cannot change and concentrate on the things we can. If you'd prefer not to repeatedly list permanent or long-range "uncontrollables," such as compulsions, obsessions, and so on, try writing "I am powerless over the usual things and . . ." Then add any specific worries or problems, such as your son's SAT scores or whether or not your sweetheart calls.

Write and Flush (or Burn)

When you're furious, feel resentments building up inside you, or otherwise need to get something off your chest without involving and potentially hurting other people or making yourself vulnerable to retribution, let your pencil do the talking. Write everything you would say if you could. Be as vindictive, childish, cruel, or ridiculous as you wish.

When your emotional energy is spent and your feelings are down on paper, reread what you've written. If you are alone and feel that you need to, read your writing out loud. *Then get rid of it.* Tear it into little pieces and toss it in the trash. Burn it. Flush it down the toilet—unless that's a bit too symbolic for those of you who used to induce vomiting. Affirm that, for now, you are through with this matter and the emotions surrounding it and are serenely and abstinently getting on with your day.

CHAPTER ELEVEN

Dealing with Feelings

"I was always fine," says Fran, a thirty-eight-year-old social worker and recovering overeater. "Just fine. *Only* fine. I had painful experiences, disappointments, rejections, but the feelings were filtered out." Or explained away.

When the community mental health center where she'd carved herself a comfortable niche as a supervisor eliminated her position, Fran barely flinched. "Of course, I wish they hadn't," she'd stated matter-of-factly at the time, "but it's probably for the best. It's giving me the push I need to get on with my life." And that was precisely—and unemotionally—what Fran did.

Likewise, when the man she'd been dating informed her that he'd met someone else, Fran was unfazed, saying, "These things happen. Naturally, I'm not *happy* about it. But the more I think about it, the more clearly I can see that he really isn't the right man for me anyway."

Less than a month later, when her stepfather died, Fran convinced herself that she had to be fine—for everyone else's sake. "The rest of my family was falling apart," she explained later. "But I managed to keep it together. I figured my turn to be upset would come after things settled down, but it never came." She considered that a blessing.

But was it? Fran managed to escape feeling grief over the loss of a loved one, pain in the wake of a rejection, and everything from fear to fury over losing her job. However, she also gained thirty pounds during the months immediately following her layoff, became obsessed with a new diet and exercise regimen right after her boyfriend dumped her, and ate virtually nonstop from the moment she got the news of her stepfather's death until she checked herself into a treatment facility nine months later.

There she learned that she wasn't "just one of those people who pretty much stay on an even keel and don't experience strong emotions."

She'd simply become so adept at automatically sweeping unpleasantness under the rug of her consciousness that she'd stopped noticing what she was feeling. Most compulsive eaters and bulimics do.

While we were caught up in our eating disorders, some of us consciously experienced few negative *or* positive emotions, preferring, as Fran did, to stay in the seemingly safe, narrow midrange of feeling "fine" or "okay." Others among us specialized in one feeling, such as anger, anxiety, or guilt. We felt that emotion, all right, and it was a powerful motivating force in our lives. A great deal of our energy went into trying to avoid it, control it, get rid of it, or atone for the things we did because of it.

"Ignorance is bliss," the saying goes, but by working overtime to ignore and push down pain, we actually kept bliss—not to mention, love, compassion, exhilaration, and serenity—beyond our grasp. We flushed the good with the bad and settled for second-rate substitutes—artificial highs or food-induced "mellows." By the time we began to extricate ourselves from our addictions, our emotional muscles had withered from disuse. We had lost faith in the part of ourselves that feels and responds to feelings appropriately. And we had little confidence in our ability to cope with any emotion of more than mild intensity.

If we want to live well and fully, our outlook will have to change. To recover emotionally, socially, and spiritually, as well as physically, we'll need to become aware of our feelings, accept all of them including the uncomfortable ones, and make decisions about what, if anything, to do about them.

Yes, That's Scary
Feeling isn't fatal. But it's tough to convince us addicts of that. After all, we've spent a significant portion of our lives treating our

emotions as if merely acknowledging them could be deadly. Surely, allowing ourselves to actually *feel* what we're feeling and (shudder) express it would demolish us on the spot. *Not true.* Feelings are never as devastating as we imagine they will be, and facing them is nowhere near as damaging as the alternative—continuing to suppress or repress our emotions and letting them fester. The resulting addictions, ulcers, heart problems, high blood pressure, and more are what can really kill us.

Feelings Are Transient

When we allow feelings to surface, they pass. Many people know this. Most food addicts don't. I was absolutely astounded the first time I was hit by a particularly powerful wave of anxiety, lay down, took a few deep breaths, waited, and discovered that, in a matter of moments, the worst of my anxiety had subsided. Yes, it would come back from time to time—and go away again as well. But so would joy, serenity, fear, sadness, compassion, anger, and excitement.

Feelings Are Not Right or Wrong, Good or Bad

Feelings, in themselves, aren't good or bad; they just are. Granted, some emotions are more unpleasant to experience than others, but all serve the same purpose—to get our attention and prompt us to examine what's going on within and around us. Feelings are signals from our inner selves, trying to make us understand something and take positive actions. By ignoring our feelings, we miss opportunities to grow and resolve problems.

Feelings Are Not Facts

Our feelings are internal reactions influenced by everything from hormone levels to our memories of similar situations. They can range in impact from mild to intense, but all feelings may seem intense to someone who hasn't experienced them in years—and they may not necessarily fit the situations in which we find ourselves.

All of us will overreact or jump to the wrong conclusions now and then. We'll decide that because we feel abandoned, we have, in fact, been abandoned or that because we're anxious, something bad actually is about to happen to us. This may not be the case, *but that doesn't mean we shouldn't feel that way.* We are each entitled to feel whatever we feel at any given moment. Indeed, we can't help but do that.

Feelings Are Reactions over Which We Have Little Real Control
We may not have as much control over our feelings as we might like, but we can control what we think and do about them. Once we allow ourselves to be aware of our feelings instead of banishing them before they reach our conscious mind, we have a whole range of options for dealing with them. We can choose to

- feel and pay attention to the feelings now
- consciously set feelings aside for a short time until we can better attend to them, such as after a crucial meeting has ended, or when our children don't need our undivided focus, or after dinner with our in-laws is over
- name our feelings
- talk or write about our feelings
- explore the circumstances and thought patterns that may have triggered the feelings
- learn something about ourselves from them
- act on them by looking for another job, changing food sponsors, introducing ourselves to someone who makes our heart flutter
- not act on them by refraining from quitting our jobs on the spot, staying in therapy, or waiting for someone we're interested in to approach us first
- relieve or release feelings through relaxation exercises, meditation, aerobic exercise, and other healthy outlets
- accept and "sit with" feelings until they pass

Start Now

Learn What You Are Feeling

After years of psychic numbing, our feelings tend to be jumbled up and virtually unidentifiable. At best, we have vague notions of feeling "bad" or "good," and some of us don't even get that far. We know that something's up simply because we feel like eating or are thinking about bingeing and purging.

Many of us also have a severely limited "feeling" vocabulary and mix up the words we do know. We say we're angry when we're actually frustrated or that we're depressed when we are merely sad. We often confuse anxiety and excitement so that even positive upcoming events seem scary or taking foolish risks seems enormously appealing.

To sort things out, *make a list of feeling words* (for example, happy, sad, frustrated, elated, worried, excited, sympathetic, angry, furious, frightened, terrified, nervous, at ease, serene, giddy, and so on) *and their meanings.* If necessary, consult a dictionary or other resources. Think about situations in which it might be appropriate or expected to feel each of the listed emotions. Recall incidents that you ate over, and identify the feelings from your list that you were probably experiencing at the time.

Start using your feeling vocabulary to label those nebulous sensations welling up from the pit of your stomach, that tightness in your chest, those butterflies or inexplicable tears. Literally stop and ask yourself what you're feeling.

Learn How to Express Emotions Safely

When you read the phrase "express emotions," you may automatically assume it means *talking* about your feelings and recoil at the mere prospect. However, emotional expression does not necessarily require conversation. It is simply the opposite of emotional *suppression.*

Instead of swallowing or numbing your emotions, let them out in ways that cause the least possible harm to yourself or others. Sometimes this involves acknowledging emotions to yourself only and then physically releasing their energy—for example, by taking a brisk walk or doing other aerobic exercise, or by crying, laughing, or punching a pillow.

Writing about feelings is helpful as well. Try recording your emotions, both positive and negative, throughout the day. Describe your emotional state and the events that preceded it. This gives you practice tuning in to and naming your feelings. It also reveals the sorts of thought patterns or circumstances that seem most likely to stir up those emotions and, as a result, paves the way for change.

As insightful and at times comforting as putting our emotions down on paper can be, we'll still need to share our feelings with other people now and then. Talking to other people about our feelings enables us to be supported, to learn that others have survived similar emotions, to hear that we are not crazy for feeling what we do, and to see that we'll continue to be accepted even after we've admitted to feeling a "bad" emotion like anger or jealousy.

It also becomes possible to begin resolving problems and conflicts instead of repeating them or creating new ones—which is what we do when we are emotionally dishonest with others or bottle up our feelings until we explode.

Please note that when I refer to sharing feelings, I do not mean indiscriminately venting them or being emotionally honest with everyone. Although some of us will inadvertently go to those extremes at first and have to make amends later, it is generally best to do the following:

- Pick out a few people who seem supportive and understanding. Share your feelings with them in small doses. If they listen and *don't* judge, give unsolicited advice, negate or minimize your feelings, or betray your confidences, share more. If they can't fulfill those prerequisites, don't make confidants of them.

- Ask yourself what you want to accomplish by discussing your feelings. Do you merely want to get them off your chest? Or do you want someone to take your side or let you know that you're okay? You may be interested in sorting through your feelings, understanding what's behind them, or deciding what to do in response to them. Once you have an inkling about what you're after, let your confidant know. Without that information, he or she might try to calm you when you need to get your anger out or try to problem-solve when what you're looking for is insight—and the conversation might leave you feeling frustrated instead of supported.

- Remember that other people are entitled to their feelings, too, including those stirred up by the ones you've shared with them. Don't dump and run, especially when you're expressing emotions related to something the other person did or also cares about, such as your marriage. Be willing to listen or, if you do walk out, to come back and clean up your mess later.

Dealing with Anger

Anger is a hostile response to anyone or anything that threatens our self-esteem or thwarts our efforts to get something we want or need. It is a desire to fight back, inflict pain, or express outrage, and arises when we encounter opposition, experience frustration, are hurt by someone, or feel cornered.

Many of us used to suppress our anger at all times. As Miriam, a recovering bulimic who had been physically and verbally abused through much of her childhood, puts it, "I was always afraid that if I lost my temper, I'd lose control completely, the way my dad did. I'd wind up hurting someone badly, maybe even killing them. That's how dangerous I thought anger was." She could not allow herself to feel it.

"I pushed it down and pushed it down, but my anger wouldn't go away," Miriam recalls. "It just kept burning inside me." Eating seemed to douse the flames. Purging provided additional relief, especially when Miriam was so angry that she felt she would explode.

Of course, some of us *did* explode—regularly and repeatedly. We used to indiscriminately lash out at every target, regardless of the consequences. Our repertoire included tantrums, scathing criticism, even violence or destruction of property, as well as forms of "cold" anger, such as giving people the silent treatment, withholding sex or affection, giving looks that could kill, and so on. Although anyone was fair game, those most likely to feel the heat of our anger were people who intentionally or accidentally hit our sore spots—our weight or eating habits.

"Heaven help anyone who tried to come between me and my 'supply,' " says Hal, a forty-year-old salesman and recovering overeater. "After thinking about my next binge for hours ahead of time, I wasn't about to let someone delay or interrupt it." He would blow up at them, almost always feeling guilty afterward. "But I was too ashamed or too afraid of getting blasted in return to apologize," Hal says. "I usually acted as if my outburst had never happened."

Not surprisingly, people learned to keep their distance from him. The guilt and shame Hal felt after he vented his anger, along with the isolation he experienced, gave him additional reasons to do more of what he was already doing too much of—eating himself into a stupor.

Still others among us neither fully suppressed nor immediately expressed our anger. Instead we converted it into resentment or bitterness that we carried around with us for years or directed at ourselves and became depressed. Fortunately, we can learn to deal with anger productively by

- recognizing when we are getting angry
- acknowledging our anger as soon as we recognize it
- consciously suppressing our anger for the time being
- discharging angry energy nonviolently
- making amends as soon as possible after losing our temper

Recognize When You Are Getting Angry

Although anger often seems to burst out of nowhere and immediately rage out of control, our minds and bodies actually send us advance warning of a pending explosion. If we train ourselves to recognize and pay attention to those clues, we increase our options for dealing with the situation that is angering us.

Some early signals of anger are a knot or burning sensation in your stomach, muscles tightening in your jaw or neck, your hands closing into fists, your face flushing, tears stinging your eyes, rapid or shallow breathing, skin tingling, an adrenaline rush, your entire body feeling so energized that you have trouble sitting still, difficulty concentrating, and thoughts like "This stinks," "That's unfair," "How dare she!" or "Who gave him the right to . . . ?"

Think back to a time when you felt that you were treated unfairly or realized that you might be prevented from accomplishing something you wanted to do, and check the symptoms you remember experiencing. Then begin looking for those symptoms when you encounter provocative *situations*. If getting angry frightens you, practice on situations that you can respond to freely (getting caught in traffic or watching your least favorite politician spout off on TV).

Acknowledge Your Anger as Soon as You Recognize It

Tell yourself, *I'm beginning to feel angry,* or *There's something going on here that is starting to tick me off.* This brings the feeling into your conscious awareness while you still have plenty of control over your behavior.

Then you can *conscientiously express anger*—which is not the same thing as indiscriminately venting it. Your goal should be to resolve whatever circumstance provoked your anger, not to blast someone with both barrels, inflict pain, or get revenge. If you catch yourself early enough, you should be able to do the following:

- Frankly inform the person that he or she has hit a nerve or that something about the interaction is getting to you. Talk about what you think may be angering you to see if you might have misunderstood or misinterpreted the other person's remarks. Discuss ways to remedy the situation. (See Resolving Conflicts, pages 195-199.) This is particularly beneficial when the other person is someone with whom you have an ongoing relationship that you'd like to keep as healthy as possible.
- Calmly, but without mincing words, share your feeling and

request that a specific behavior be discontinued. This option works well during brief or one-time interactions when the other person's words or actions are clearly inappropriate, such as when a colleague bursts into your office without knocking, a sales clerk is rude to you, or your four-year-old smacks you in the face with her shoe. (See pages 195-196 for a particularly effective technique to use in such situations.)

Consciously Suppress Your Anger for the Time Being

In certain situations, it is not in your best interest to express anger openly and directly—for instance, if you're angry at a boss who might fire you, surrounded by onlookers with whom you'd prefer not to share your private business, interacting with someone who might become violent, or simply not given an opportunity to respond. When you encounter such circumstances and have acknowledged your anger to yourself, it is perfectly okay to push those feelings aside *temporarily*. The trick is to do this consciously, then find a healthy outlet for your anger and, as soon as possible, use it to get your feelings out into the open.

Discharge Angry Energy Nonviolently

Suppressed anger builds like steam in a boiler. When the pressure reaches a certain level, it has to be released. Venting anger with no holds barred provides that release—which is why people do it. For people who suppress anger over extended periods of time, it escapes in other ways—through physical illnesses or passive-aggressive behavior such as lateness, "forgetting" to do things that are important to the person with whom they are angry, or "accidentally" destroying that person's property. Following are some far healthier methods for discharging anger:

- Talk about the incident with someone who wasn't involved in it.
- Write about the incident. Really let yourself go. Write down everything you wish you could have said and any revenge fantasies you have. You can destroy this scathing document or

keep it to read at a later date and learn more about what makes you angry and why.

- Release angry energy physically. Punch a pillow. Get in your car, roll up the windows, and scream at the top of your lungs. Shut yourself up in the bathroom and jog in place or jump up and down. Fling a beanbag or tennis ball against the nearest wall. Turn on your stereo and dance until you're ready to drop.

Once angry energy dissipates, you generally will see that in addition to being angry, you were feeling hurt or frightened. In fact, anger is almost always a defense against those primary emotions. We fly into rages, give people the silent treatment, or go on and on about how furious we are to avoid confronting how much a remark hurt us or how afraid we are of losing someone's love or approval.

That is why you also may want to consider removing yourself from a provocative situation temporarily. If need be, excuse yourself to use the rest room. During your time-out, release some of your angry energy, try to pinpoint the underlying wound or fear, and, if appropriate, bring it up for discussion when you return.

Make Amends As Soon As Possible After Losing Your Temper

Your anger may have been justified, but your tantrum probably did more harm than good. Clean up the mess—even if it means humbling yourself or withstanding a few angry words hurled in your direction. If you have to interact with that person again in the future, it is wise to attempt to reach an understanding about the circumstances that set off your outburst. Remember, effectively dealing with anger is not just getting it out of your system, but also taking steps to resolve the conflict or problem behind it.

Managing Anxiety

Anxiety is a fear of what *might* happen, a sense of distress or uneasiness in response to a real, imagined, or perceived threat to our safety, sanity, or self-esteem. *Uh oh*, we think, *here comes danger . . . misfortune . . . circumstances I'll be unable to change . . . accept . . .*

control . . . cope with. . . . and whether or not that assessment has any basis in reality, an alarm sounds in our psyche. We become tense, ready for a fight, or poised to take flight—with escape of some sort often being the preferred option. The heart beats faster, the mouth gets dry, and the stomach turns somersaults. We are possessed by an overwhelming sense of dread, nervousness, and extreme discomfort.

Anxiety can be incredibly uncomfortable, and although no one likes discomfort, those of us prone to eating disorders and other addictions seem to have an exceptionally low tolerance for it. We have a powerful need to make any discomfort go away the instant we feel it and may have gone to great lengths to prevent ourselves from feeling any anxiety at all, ever. We reached for the chips or chocolate as soon as we suspected we might become anxious.

We overplanned, overworried, and became overprotective, turning into intolerable control freaks who seemed to think we would ward off disaster if we could just compel everyone and everything to conform to our expectations. Or, intent upon avoiding any object or activity that might provoke an anxiety attack, we retreated from life almost entirely. If something seemed the least bit dangerous, we stayed away from it. Food filled the void, and feeling fat provided the excuse to stay out of anxiety-provoking situations even longer.

All of those strategies ultimately proved to be counterproductive; for anxiety, like all emotions, is not good, bad, or deadly. It is a signal that something is brewing, specifically that circumstances we are about to encounter or something we're thinking of doing could have painful consequences. Without that signal, we'd be at the mercy of our impulses and vulnerable to all of the world's real dangers, such as oncoming traffic, muggers, eviction, irate spouses, and so on.

Even when threats are coming from unknown or largely imaginary sources, our anxious feelings have something to show or teach us. By smothering them with food, we missed out on an opportunity to learn something about ourselves or the world around us that could have helped us more effectively deal with other anxiety-provoking circumstances. Lacking that know-how, we became more anxious in more situations and more driven to keep our anxiety buried under a mountain of food.

Like anger, anxiety can be dealt with in a number of productive ways. The next pages will discuss these options:

- Give yourself permission to be anxious now and then.
- Use relaxation and guided imagery techniques.
- Figure out what you can do, picture yourself doing it, and do it.

Give Yourself Permission to Be Anxious Now and Then

When we're facing life without our favorite coping mechanism and tackling things we never got through without overeating or bingeing and purging, there's a lot to be anxious about. Indeed, with past dieting failures causing us to predict more of the same, recovery itself—especially becoming and staying physically abstinent—is anxiety-provoking.

In addition, free-floating anxiety, the kind that strikes for no apparent reason and causes us to seriously question our sanity, is commonplace for those of us who spent a lifetime cutting ourselves off from our emotions. With virtually no previous experience in connecting our feelings to the circumstances that aroused them, we have only the vaguest notion of what might be making us anxious now. But that doesn't mean that we're coming completely unhinged.

Unexplainable anxiety is not a sign of insanity. Telling ourselves that it is, that we shouldn't feel it, or that we must be losing our mind only makes matters worse. And that goes for explainable anxiety too. The more harshly we judge anxious feelings, yell at ourselves for having them, or worry about what might happen if they don't stop soon, the more anxious we'll become.

So try not to fight the feeling. Acknowledge it. Allow it. (Think: "It's okay to be anxious now. It's to be expected under these circumstances.") Normalize it. (Think: "Everyone feels this way sometimes. It's part of being human—and it passes." If possible, come up with a specific example from the life of a friend or colleague.) Accept the feeling and either wait it out or go on with what you were doing even though you are still feeling it.

If we don't poke and pick at anxiety's distressing symptoms like scabs on a scraped knee, they will subside. Mild anxiety tends to subside naturally. Moderate or intense anxiety may need a little of your help.

Use Relaxation and Guided Imagery Techniques

Take fifteen to twenty minutes when you are not particularly anxious and do the following:

1. Relax using the deep muscle technique (found on pages 121-122) or any other method you'd prefer.
2. Visualize a calm scene. Just float with it until you feel at ease. Your anxiety level is now at zero.
3. Switch your mental focus to someone or something that typically makes you anxious. (But don't select the most anxiety-provoking thing in your life. Remember, this is just practice.) As you think about this individual or event, you'll notice your anxiety increasing. When it reaches approximately a three on a zero-to-ten scale. . . .
4. Take several slow, deep breaths and once again visualize a calm scene. Don't fight any anxious thoughts or images that remain. Simply note their presence, mentally nod to them, and return your focus to your breathing and your calm scene. Stay with this until your anxiety level has returned to zero.
5. Repeat steps two, three, and four several times, allowing your anxiety level to rise further with each repetition. Make sure you're back down to zero (and throw in a few affirmations) before you open your eyes.

Your practice sessions with this technique will dramatically demonstrate the fact that you can lower your anxiety level at will. Once you've developed some confidence in your ability to do it, start using the technique when you're actually feeling anxious. Try to catch yourself at a level of five or below, but even if you've skyrocketed to an eight or a nine, relax your body, your breathing, and your mind until your anxiety passes or subsides sufficiently to allow you to resume your previous activity.

This technique also can be used for *desensitization*. Choose an anxiety-provoking situation that you encounter regularly and would like to stop getting so worked up over. Make it your focus for a week or so of daily practice sessions. First, you'll notice that it becomes more difficult to mentally increase your anxiety over that once-dreaded circumstance. Eventually, you'll find yourself feeling less anxious about it when it happens in real life.

Like anger, anxiety can also be discharged physically. Talking helps too, and laughter is also an anxiety-buster.

Figure Out What You Can Do, Picture Yourself Doing It, and Do It
No matter how we try, none of us will eliminate anxious feelings completely—nor should we. However, instead of literally worrying ourselves sick over potential problems, we can prepare for them by identifying and planning the measures we'll take if our anxious imaginings actually should be realized.

Start by dissecting the anxiety-provoking situation. Think it through. What could go wrong during tomorrow's meeting with a belligerent employee? What calamities could occur during that dreaded family reunion? How bad could the singles' function or giving a speech in front of one hundred people be? List your fears and worries; then divide your list into three categories:

- *Farfetched fears or low-probability outcomes*. Worrying that the employee will grab you by the throat and choke the life out of you fits into this category. Draw a line through these entries. Cross them out in your mind too.

- *Unwelcome but tolerable turn of events*. Walking around at the family reunion nervously awaiting an argument to occur fits in this category. That family fighting has been part of every reunion for the past twenty years. It hasn't killed you yet. Although the experience may not be pleasant, you know you can get through it. Circle these items. Plan to use anxiety-

lowering techniques to decrease your discomfort as needed.
- *Outcomes that could be prevented, more easily tolerated, or more effectively handled—if you had some sort of action plan for dealing with them.* Put a star (*) beside each of these.

For each starred item, identify at least one action you could take if that negative event actually occurred. It doesn't have to be the perfect comeback line or a wonderfully courageous act. For instance, excusing yourself to use the rest room may seem like a cowardly or dishonest way to escape the clutches of an overly attentive man in a singles bar, but it works—and you can do it without taking a ten-week course in assertiveness.

Like everything else in the recovery process, these contingency plans tend to be most effective when you keep them simple, and sometimes the simplest thing is to do nothing overt. Smiling (or deep breathing) and saying nice things to yourself is a powerful action in an anxiety-provoking situation. In addition, just *making* backup plans can reduce anxiety. It is reassuring to know what you could do if the worst happened. And it boosts your self-esteem to realize that you actually have many of the coping skills you need. Visualizing yourself using those skills can ease your mind and build your confidence even further.

Using a guided imagery technique like the one described earlier in this section, mentally walk yourself through the event you've been apprehensive about. Picture yourself in the thick of it. See yourself encountering the trouble you predicted and *using your backup plan to handle it.* If new obstacles show up during the visualization, imagine yourself dealing with them (taking an effective action) or coping with them (acknowledging their existence, but not letting them get to you). If your anxiety rises above a level you can comfortably tolerate, use deep breathing or focusing on a calm scene to lower it.

You may want to picture different outcomes for different purposes—for instance, the best possible results to encourage yourself; a realistic worst-case scenario to show yourself that you'd live through it; or an acceptable—although not necessarily great—ending to keep your expectations close to reality. I also recommend visualizing yourself one hour, day, or week *after* the event feeling relaxed, serene, and self-confident—regardless of the outcome.

Bolstered by this imagery (and perhaps a few reminders about your past successes), get out there and face that anxiety-provoking situation. It probably won't turn out exactly as you visualized it, but I guarantee that it will be a heck of a lot better than the catastrophe you predicted would occur when you were stuck in "needless worry" mode.

Conquering Fear

Most of us won't have to look up the definition of fear in the dictionary. We know it well. We know it as heart-pounding, head-throbbing, stomach-churning, pulse-racing agony. And we know it intimately. It's been a near-constant companion to some of us and a driving force in many of our lives.

Fear has compelled us to run and hide or try in any way we can to escape and avoid whatever frightens us. Fear has prevented us from taking the risks that would have shown us we had less to fear. We have engaged in countless eat-a-thons, desperation diets, and binge/purge cycles to quiet our fears or to divert our attention from them, or both. And fear will make our recovery almost as nightmarish as our eating disorders—if we let it.

What Fear Has Us Do—or Not Do

Needless to say, we used to overeat or binge and purge when we were afraid—often before we consciously felt our fear. And even after we are in recovery, we may remain in the dark about what truly frightens us by allowing fear of relapse to become the driving force in our lives.

In addition, we probably used virtually everyone's first choice in coping strategies—avoidance. We simply stayed away from the things that frightened us. We thought this strategy worked because our lack of contact with frightening people, places, and things did indeed reduce the number of painful experiences we had.

However, in addition to the other things fear made us do, it also limited or entirely eliminated our chances of experiencing success, satisfaction, acceptance, intimacy, or many other things that could have enhanced our self-esteem, refuted our negative beliefs, and reduced our fear. While we were avoiding the calamities we feared, we were missing the accomplishments, closeness, and fun that could have made our lives fulfilling.

In the following pages, I'll discuss what we can do to counteract our fears. The strategies include

- Getting acquainted with your fears
- Getting real
- Getting busy

Getting Acquainted with Your Fears

Several years ago, I attended a seminar in which fear was described as a monster in a cave. At some point in our lives, we walked past that cave, and the monster jumped out and pounced on us, inflicting enough pain to convince us to steer clear of the cave in the future. We continue to steer clear of it—*even though we haven't actually seen the monster in ages*. We assume it's still in there, that it will still pounce on us, and that the pain will be at least as bad as, if not worse than, it was before. But that may not be true. In fact, most of the time it isn't.

Our fears may be linked to events that took place when we were young or to more recent occurrences that took us by surprise. They aren't happening now. Under similar circumstances today, the same thing might not happen again. Even if it did, it probably wouldn't be as painful, because we now have more knowledge, skill, or support and could deal with it more effectively. We might come through the experience unscathed. But our unconscious doesn't know that—and it's churning up the lion's share of our fear.

Over the years, we've fertilized our fears with negative self-talk and unfavorable comparisons of ourselves to other people. As a result, the fears have been magnified and distorted in our mind's eye. But we don't recognize that. Because our habit of avoiding frightening situations prevented us from having practical experiences to counteract our perceptions, we don't know that they are faulty. We don't realize that the things that scare us really aren't as scary as they seem. However, we can become more realistic about them now. By shining a light in that cave and taking a look at what's really lurking there, we can cut our fears down to size and learn to respect them without being dominated by them.

Try talking to your fear. Picture it in human (or monster) form, sitting right in front of you and conversing with you. Take out your journal, and write the dialogue you'd have. Here's an example:

FEAR: I'm back.

SELF: I noticed. Why are you here?

FEAR: Because you need me.

SELF: I think not.

FEAR: Well, think again. Think about what would happen if I weren't around to protect you.

SELF: Protect me? You're making me miserable.

FEAR: Not as miserable as you'd be if I didn't stop you from doing dumb, dangerous things.

SELF: Like what?

FEAR: Like trusting that guy you've been seeing or believing he could actually stay interested in you for long. He's going to find someone better and dump you the first chance he gets. . . .

Let the conversation go where it will—over painful past experiences, personal sore spots, embarrassing moments, or long-standing insecurities. Feel free to debate and disagree with your fear as well.

SELF: You're talking about stuff that happened in the past.

FEAR: Of course I am. I want you to remember how hurt and disappointed you were and how you did nothing but cry and eat for days. Then you stopped crying but kept on eating until you weighed over two hundred pounds.

SELF: Then I didn't have to worry about someone dumping me

because I was too gross for anyone to approach in the first place.

FEAR: Yes, and I convinced you not to go anyplace where you might meet someone either. Those were the days. You really listened to me back then. None of this turning-me-over-to-a-Higher-Power garbage.

SELF: But that's *my* point. I was too young to know better then. I didn't have recovery. I didn't understand myself or know how to cope as well as I do now. . . .

Refuting fear's arguments gives you the courage to consider going ahead with what you've been afraid to do. When you reach that point in your dialogue, say so. You also might try asking your fear for some reasonable advice about protecting yourself from any realistic dangers your undertaking could present. Fear is not all bad. Its value simply gets lost when we overdramatize it, overreact to it, or confuse feelings with fact.

Getting Real

Like other emotions, fear draws attention to something that is actually going on within or around you, but it rarely if ever accurately represents those conditions or events. Just reread your dialogue with fear, and you'll quickly see that it's loaded with untruths, like the following:

- *Transferred feelings*—Fear and other emotions connected to something that hurt or scared you in the past. They may have little or no relevance to your current circumstances and, even when applicable, are more intense than the realities of the present situation dictate.

- *Trend-spotting*—Fear that a negative event is going to repeat itself endlessly. "In the past, guys I liked dumped me, so this one will too," or "Every time I applied for a job I really wanted, I didn't get it, so I'd only be setting myself up for disappointment if I applied for this one."

- *Globalizing*—Seeing a single incident as something that *always* happens to you, one person's reaction as something *everyone* must think about you, and so on.

- *Catastrophizing*—Conjuring up the worst possible outcomes for any situation that has the slightest possibility of turning out unfavorably.

Thought patterns like these intensify your fears and weaken your resolve to act in your own behalf or stick to a previously chosen course of action. When you spot them in your writings or hear them running through your mind, try to come up with more reasonable, realistic ideas or interpretations. (For how-tos, see Rethinking, pages 146-149.)

Or try using your tendency to look on the dark side to your advantage. When you're in a situation or facing a challenge that frightens you, ask yourself: "What's the worst thing that could happen?" Then go ahead and catastrophize. Share your worst-case scenarios with a friend, or write them down. You'll immediately see how absurd some of them are and how unlikely it is that they would come to pass. If you can find even two or three that could actually happen, you'll discover, more often than not, that the worst is not so bad, that you have the capabilities to cope with it, and that the impact of it would probably cause less agony than living in fear of it has.

This realization should boost your confidence and courage. But will it make your fear go away? Usually not. To truly conquer a fear—and know how good it feels to get rid of one—you'll need to directly confront it. You'll need to *take risks*, to reach for probable success, healing, growth, and other gifts of recovery even though doing so may expose you to the possibility of failure, pain, loss, and other feared outcomes.

Getting Busy

Prepare to take new risks by reminding yourself of the ones you've already taken that turned out well. You'll be amazed at how many there are. You wouldn't be a friend or be raising children, holding down a job, working a program of recovery, or doing almost anything else if you hadn't risen to a challenge or faced down a fear at some point in the past. Start a "Risks Taken" list, and add to it each time you take a new one.

Identify the factors that made past risks easier to take. Who or what helped you get over hurdles that once may have seemed insurmountable? The encouragement of a friend? The skepticism of a colleague? Giving yourself a pep talk? Perhaps you found a buddy to participate in the risky endeavor along with you or arranged to give yourself some sort of reward for going through with it. The motivators that worked then can work for you again. Consider putting similar supports into place before you take your next risk.

When taking new risks, start small. List some risks you'd like to take. They may be things you've always wanted to do but were afraid to try, such as wind surfing or taking a creative writing course; things you need to do but tend to avoid (such as making amends to a friend you hurt while caught up in your food addiction or finally getting rid of your fat clothes); or simply fears you'd like to conquer, like speaking in front of a group or returning purchases to department stores.

As you can tell from my examples, all the items on your list need not be major tests of courage or actions that would dramatically change your life. In fact, make sure to include a number of small-fry risks, and plan to take them first. If you haven't faced many fears or risen to any challenges lately, you'll need the practice. By experiencing success—or discovering that you can survive failure—in areas that aren't particularly emotion-charged or life-altering, you gain confidence for taking bigger, more frightening risks.

Be selective. Whether big or small, it pays to know a good risk from a bad one and when to walk away or wait awhile rather than forging ahead against all odds. I recommend applying the cost/benefit analysis I described on pages 126-127 to the risk you're considering taking. If the potential positive outcomes of taking a particular risk at a particular time outweigh the possible negative repercussions, it's probably safe to go ahead with it.

Visualize yourself taking the risk. If you can't tolerate thinking about it, chances are that you aren't ready to go through with it. However, you can increase your tolerance by using the relaxation and anxiety-reducing guided imagery techniques found on pages 121-123 and 170-171. Writing out a script and mentally rehearsing it help too, as do creating and reciting affirmations.

Finally, keep in mind that the highest level of fear generally occurs right before you jump. Once you're involved in actually taking a risk, your fear subsides, so when the moment of truth arrives, just take a deep breath and go for it. You'll be fine. And you'll be starting a positive cycle. By taking risks, you reduce fear and enhance self-esteem, which makes it easier to take more risks, conquer more fears, and feel even better about yourself.

CHAPTER TWELVE

Relate to Recover

"I've been a loner all my life," claims Darlene, a thirty-four-year-old recovering compulsive eater. "I was an only child, so I was alone a lot to begin with. But when I was eight, my mother went back to work full-time, and I was alone even more." Every day, from 3:30 when school let out until 6:30 when her mother got home, Darlene was completely on her own.

Each morning her mother would prepare a tray of special treats for her daughter to snack on during the time she'd be alone. "Maybe she thought that would make up for her not being there," Darlene says. It didn't, but she did eat everything her mother left for her, and then some. She ate out of boredom and loneliness, because she felt empty inside and isolated from the outside world—all of which increased when she hit her teens.

"I didn't date," she recalls. "I didn't hang out with anyone. While other kids my age were at dances and basketball games, I was at home playing pinochle with my parents or curled up in bed with a book." And eating. Her weight climbed into the 180s. Feeling awkward and inferior when opportunities to be with her peers did arise, Darlene rarely took advantage of them. "I thought people invited me places because they felt sorry for me," she notes. "Or I convinced myself that putting myself in certain situations was just asking to be laughed at or ostracized. After all, who really wants to be with a fat girl?"

Darlene promised herself that she'd get out more once she got down to a lower weight. But like other compulsive eaters, her diets were doomed to fail. "I'd be fine during the day," she says.

"But when nighttime rolled around and I was alone, lonely, and miserable, I'd head straight for the cookie jar or corner deli." This pattern persisted through her college years and her postgraduation move to a new city where she knew no one and couldn't seem to click with her co-workers.

Darlene was shocked when a man she met during a behavior modification class at a quick-weight-loss clinic took an interest in her. "I couldn't understand what Ralph saw in me," she says. "But I liked the attention and the idea of being part of a pair, instead of on my own all the time." After less than six months of once-a-week dating, Ralph proposed, and even though she still couldn't believe anyone would want to make that kind of commitment to her, Darlene agreed to marry him. However, being married did little to relieve her sense of isolation—or curtail her compulsive eating.

"Ralph turned out to be a workaholic," she says. "He was out of town on business three or four days every week, and when he was home, he spent most of his time holed up in his study doing paperwork or talking on the telephone." But that really didn't bother her, Darlene insisted. Prior to embarking on a program of recovery fourteen months ago, she was more into food than conversation, sex, or anything else Ralph could offer her. "Sometimes I was actually glad he wasn't around," she notes, "because it meant I could eat as much as I wanted of anything I wanted without being interrupted or criticized for it."

Food addiction is a disease of isolation. Like Darlene, we used food and compulsive behavior to fill the emotional voids in our lives and drown out our yearning for closeness, camaraderie, and meaningful human contact. Then, as our compulsion to overeat or binge and purge began to take precedence over everything else in our lives—including our relationships—we *isolated ourselves* in order to continue our addictive behavior and ensure that we weren't found out, ridiculed, humiliated, or coerced into changing.

Once a gregarious, straight-A student, active in sports and popular with her peers, Emily, a twenty-five-year-old recovering bulimic, found less and less time for friendship or dating as her eating disorder progressed.

"I had no use for people when my mind was locked in on my next binge," she admits. "I definitely didn't want them around when I was eating or vomiting or working out like a madwoman. And I couldn't think of anything worse than having my friends or family figure out what I was up to." They would be as disgusted with her as she was with herself, she thought, and she'd feel completely humiliated. Or they would try to make her stop what she'd been doing and she'd become "a big bloated blob" overnight. Either fate was unthinkable. So Emily turned down invitations, preferring to stay home and eat, and snapped at anyone who seemed curious about her life.

The people around Emily got her message and responded accordingly. Soon there was no one around when she *did* want to be with people, and the resulting loneliness—and regret—only fueled the emotional uproar Emily binged and purged to douse.

Eating disorders, loneliness, and relationship difficulties always walk hand in hand. Whether we experienced it before or after we began abusing food, all of us have felt disconnected, drastically different from other people, trapped behind invisible walls that kept us from getting close to anyone, or utterly alone—even in a crowd.

The isolation that perpetuates and is perpetuated by our food addiction is not always physical. In fact, many of us have spent a good deal of our lives substituting food for the love, acceptance, and emotional support we weren't getting from people—even though there were plenty of them around us.

The first few times that Max, a fifty-eight-year-old recovering overeater, heard people at OA meetings talk about the link between loneliness and compulsive eating, he found it difficult to grasp the concept or apply it to his own life. "I'm anything but isolated," he had declared at the time. "And there's no way I'm overeating because I lack human contact. If you ask me, I have too much of it." As a foster parent for delinquent adolescents, an outspoken advocate for children in general, and an active member of his church and community, Max was, as he put it, "up to my eyeballs in people, all of them pushing and pulling and needing something from me."

"But how many of those people do you really feel close to and comfortable with?" his sponsor asked, and Max had to admit that only a handful would fall into that category. He could rarely relax and let his hair down around any of them, he realized, and didn't seek them out when he felt blue, frustrated, or confused. What's more, he couldn't even imagine them listening or understanding him if he did.

"Psychologically speaking, I really was alone," Max now sighs. "Almost all of my relationships were one-way streets." Each time the tender, loving care Max so freely gave wasn't reciprocated, *he took care of himself* by feeding himself. Did you?

Whether we were ashamed of our appearance or interested in concealing our behavior, determined to lose weight before venturing into new social situations or, like Max, busy taking care of everyone but ourselves, we cut ourselves off from other people. And whether we convinced ourselves that we preferred to be alone or knew all too well that we didn't, deep inside we felt a desire to belong, a longing for the presence of other human beings and meaningful interactions with them. We were lonely. But like most lonely people—both those with eating disorders and those without—rather than admitting our loneliness and taking action to relieve it, we tended to isolate further, increase it, and become more dependent on the substances and activities that helped us forget it.

Of all the vicious cycles in our lives, this is one of the most difficult to discontinue. Even before our eating disorders got the better of us, most of us were extremely sensitive to social norms and what other people thought of us. Many of us were self-conscious in social situations and inclined to distance ourselves from people. And the longer we did, the more anxious and insecure about getting close to them we became.

Now we may not know how to break the ice, make small talk or get beyond it, or relate to others in anything but our roles as caretakers or "entertainers." The concept that anyone could like to be with us may be an alien one. As a result, merely feeling attracted to someone can set off internal alarms that make us want to turn tail and run. Or we may act as if we shouldn't need people and try to do without them because we're convinced that longing for camaraderie and others' support is a sign of weakness or a surefire prescription for disappointment.

But the need for closeness and meaningful human interaction is a legitimate one. It is an integral, inescapable part of being human, and the ability to fulfill it in healthy, positive ways is essential for long-term recovery.

Come Out of Isolation

Put Yourself in Places Where There Are People You'd Like to Know

As I've noted in earlier chapters, if you're looking for accepting, like-minded men and women, Twelve Step recovery or other support groups offer an excellent starting point. In fact, there are few places where you'll have a better chance of meeting people who can understand you and are willing to take you as you are. However, the connections you make in recovery groups may not provide all of the closeness you need.

Differences in age, marital status, work schedules, and interests may limit socializing outside meetings. Or you simply may want to expand your circle of friends. You can meet potentially compatible people and improve the odds that you will click with them by identifying activities that interest you and going to where those activities take place.

Start a list of things you'd like to do for fun . . . for learning . . . to be of service in your community . . . to enhance your spirituality . . . to get some exercise. Then pull out the Yellow Pages or ask around to find out where you can do those things. If you don't want to go alone or feel you'll need the moral support, ask a friend, relative, or acquaintance to accompany you. Then start participating. In an environment that interests you and ignites your enthusiasm, you'll find people naturally being drawn to you.

Once There, Reach Out

While caught up in my eating disorder, I was like Max. I had plenty of people around me but only one or two with whom I could open up and be myself. When I was ready to change that, I took my own advice, got out of the house, placed myself in situations conducive to meeting people—and immediately hit a major roadblock. I couldn't bring myself to say more than a few words to anyone.

Even at OA meetings, I felt that by reaching out to people, I was somehow bothering them. I preferred to have them approach me. But when they did, I fell back into my familiar helper role and listened to their concerns without revealing my own. I had to break out of that rut, I realized, and to do it, I needed to work on my attitude and sharpen my conversational skills. You may need to also.

First, before entering any social situation or one-on-one interaction, make a conscious effort to turn off the tape of negative self-talk that tends to play and replay itself in your mind. Most of those messages are obsolete or make-believe anyway. Replace them with positive affirmations.

Second, expect acceptance. Instead of walking into parties, meetings, and such, thinking about being ignored, rejected, or ridiculed—as so many of us do—tell yourself that the people you're going to meet are going to accept you. Most of the time, they actually want to. They aren't standing around looking for something to dislike about you. Remind yourself of your positive attributes and accomplishments. Think about how you'd act if you already knew that others liked you, and then act that way.

Third, be a chooser. Many of us, because of the low self-esteem that is part and parcel of our eating disorders, have fallen into the habit of finding a safe spot at any gathering, standing in it as if our feet were nailed to the floor, and waiting for someone to approach us. We barely make eye contact with the people we hope will come our way yet feel more nervous and dejected with each moment that passes without someone wonderful noticing us.

If we don't give up and go home, swearing never to set foot in that particular place again, we end up gratefully accepting the attention of *anyone* who shows the least bit of interest in us. This passive approach to socializing does nothing to boost our confidence or convince us to continue trying to connect with people.

Although it can be anxiety-provoking, especially for those of you who are extra-sensitive to rejection, you'll fare better by selecting the people *you* want to meet or converse with and making the first move. It doesn't have to be a showstopper. Smile. Make eye contact. Say hello. Introduce yourself. Then ask a simple, straightforward, here-and-now question, such as "What did you think of the speech?" or "How are you enjoying the party?" or "This is my first time at one of these conferences. How about you?"

Really listen to the other person's answer—and try not to worry about what you'll say next. Take your cue from what you're hearing. Ask a related question, or share your own impressions. Describe ideas or experiences of your own that are similar to those mentioned by the person with whom you're talking. And if something that person does or says intrigues, amuses, or impresses you, say so. You'll be conveying respect, warmth, and acceptance as well as letting him or her know that you're paying attention—and that's a message everyone enjoys receiving.

If your conversation gets stuck, try asking more questions. If it never gets off the ground, give yourself credit for trying, and then try again with someone else. Modify your approach if you think that's necessary, but realize that even with a flawless delivery, you simply won't click with everyone you meet. No one does.

Finally, *give of yourself—mindfully*. OA and other Twelve Step programs suggest that recovering individuals combat unhealthy self-centeredness and become less isolated by being of service to others. For the most part, I agree with that piece of advice. A powerful sense of belonging and usefulness can indeed be derived from helping fellow eating disorder sufferers as well as by getting involved with various community service organizations.

However, those of us who made a practice of giving and giving some more while we were eating compulsively or bingeing and purging need to be careful and even a bit self-protective when it comes to service. We can all too easily use it to avoid dealing with our own needs and issues or end up going overboard and feeling drained and resentful. Both paths tend to lead back to addictive behavior. Consequently, before choosing service as an answer to your loneliness and isolation, take a good look at the following recommendations.

Establish Boundaries

Boundaries are the invisible lines that separate and distinguish us from other people. Within our *personal* boundaries are all the things that define who we are; all the traits, quirks, strengths, and limitations that combine to make us unique and identifiable as distinct, one-of-a-kind individuals. We also have other boundaries:

- *Intimacy boundaries.* These surround the aspects of our innermost selves that we are willing to share with only a small number of people whom we fully trust.

- *Closeness boundaries.* These admit more people—friends or family members with whom we have relatively comfortable, caring, give-and-take relationships—but offer them less access to our most precious thoughts and feelings.

- *Propriety boundaries.* These govern our interactions with colleagues, clients, and casual acquaintances, allowing us to relate to them in an appropriate, even friendly manner without necessarily sharing much (or any) personal information.

- *Protective boundaries.* These go up whenever we sense that we could be hurt, betrayed, tricked, or mistreated in some way.

I have never met a compulsive overeater or bulimic who didn't have trouble in at least one of those areas.

Some of us have such fluid boundaries that we can barely tell where we end and other people begin. As far as we're concerned, all of their actions are directed at us personally. Their feelings are our responsibility. Because we can't be happy unless they are, we aim to please at all times and at any cost—including the neglect of our own needs.

Others among us have such rigid boundaries that nothing less powerful than a Sherman tank could plow through them. We're certain that anyone who gets close to us will hurt us or only wants to use us, so we keep everyone at a distance.

In addition, almost all of us in one way or another allowed our bodies or compulsions to define our boundaries for us. Walls of fat protected us from unwanted sexual attention. Our determination to lose a few more pounds or stick to our latest superstrict diet kept us out of anxiety-provoking social situations. Our bingeing and purging drove a wedge between us and parents, lovers, or friends who were crowding us in some way that we couldn't express verbally (and may not have consciously recognized). Or it had the opposite effect, grabbing their attention and bringing them closer to us as they scrambled to help with our problem.

As part of our emotional, social, and spiritual recovery, we need to establish clear, healthy boundaries that allow us to connect without losing our identity, be safe without building impenetrable barriers, and get close while retaining our self-respect and sobriety. Here's how.

Define Yourself

Who are you, anyway? What makes you unique? What are your likes and dislikes, favorite colors, music, seasons, or books? Do you have secret or not-so-secret talents . . . dreams . . . wishes? What traits have you inherited from others? Regardless of their origin, what characteristics would you like to pass on to your children? Take a cue from the curriculum guide for most kindergartens, and start an "all about me" book. Fill it with pictures, drawings, notes, and memorabilia that identify you.

Draw Lines

Take out two fairly large sheets of paper, and draw a big bull's-eye target on each. You'll need a center circle and four rings around it to correspond with the boundary categories I described earlier. Label each ring so that both diagrams look like this:

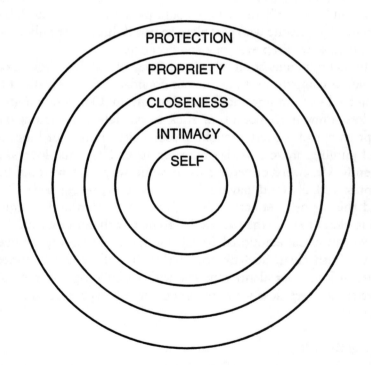

One diagram will represent the boundaries you've had up until now. The other will show the boundaries you would like to establish for yourself. Use the words *before* and *after* to signify which is which.

Then, starting with the *before* diagram, think about the kinds of information about yourself (your age, sexual preference, most embarrassing moment, fondest childhood memory, fears, vacation plans, and so on) or activities (sex, shopping, overnight visits, sharing rides, being seen without makeup, and the like) that you have traditionally relegated to each circle. What was for you only (personal boundary)? For intimates and friends (intimacy or closeness boundary)? What would you willingly reveal to or do with anyone who asked (propriety boundary)? As you come up with answers, jot them down in the appropriate ring of your *before* diagram.

In the protection circle, list the people or things from which you've traditionally tried to protect yourself (rapists, muggers, drunks, critics, bill collectors, people seeking loans or donations, commitments, know-it-alls who try to tell you how to lose weight, and so on).

Next, place the names of various people in your life in the circle they've traditionally occupied. Have you been intimate, close, or appropriate but somewhat aloof with your mother, spouse, boss, neighbor, sister, or hair stylist? Are there people in your life you go out of your way to keep from knowing you?

Then play *What's Wrong with This Picture?* Look over your *before* diagram and identify anything that seems *out of place*. Are there too many people in either your intimacy or protection circles? Do you share too much of yourself with too many or next to nothing with anyone? Would you like more people in your closeness circle or less personal data available to people in the *propriety* circle?

What about clearing out some of the entries in your protection circle so that you don't have to expend so much energy keeping your guard up? Using the same data that you charted on your *before* bull's-eye, fill in your *after* diagram to illustrate where you'd like your boundaries to be now and in the future. Then begin to establish and honor those boundaries in your daily life.

Put Distance Between Yourself and Negative, Recovery-Sabotaging People

Their attitudes and actions—from dumping their problems on you to reminding you of your past failures and warning you not to get too excited about your recent successes—are *toxic*. They poison your spirit and undermine your confidence.

The people who do that may not mean to. In fact, some of the most toxic people in our lives are the ones who, underneath it all, love and want the best for us. Others are simply reacting to conflict and confusion in their own lives. Their bitter, hypercritical, doom-and-gloom outlook has little or nothing to do with us. But it still affects us. We enhance our self-esteem—and our recovery—by taking action to limit that effect.

- *Spend less time with toxic people.* Is it really necessary to sit through tense, formal family dinners *every* week? Why not cut it down to every other week or once a month? Arrange or conjure up other engagements if begging off seems out of the question.

- *Limit their access to you.* If you need a break from listening to toxic people's troubles, turn on your answering machine. Let them know that there are certain times when it's difficult for you to concentrate on what they're saying, such as first thing in the morning or right after you get home from work, and ask them not to call at those times. Find reasons to quickly curtail conversations.

- *Pick and choose the activities you take part in together.* If your friend's bitter commentary on men makes attending singles functions with her unbearable, stop doing it. Do something else with her instead.

- *When you can't decrease physical contact, increase mental distance.* Try not to take other people's moods so personally. Stop automatically blaming yourself for them or assuming responsibility for improving them. The same goes for criticism. Train yourself to listen objectively. Agree with any truth you hear, or acknowledge that your critic *might* be right about some of what he or she is saying. Then ask yourself, "Is this criticism giving me new insights or information that will help me be more lovable, capable, or content?" If so, use it. If not, let it go.

Say No with Your Vocal Cords—Not Your Body.

Another way you can maintain the integrity of your personal boundaries is by saying no when you are asked for something you'd prefer not to give. That request may blatantly violate your boundaries (for example, being pressured for sex by someone you barely know or by a therapist or boss with whom you have a decidedly nonsexual relationship). Or it may clearly conflict with your needs, such as being asked to baby-sit on your bowling night or being urged to "just take a little taste" of something that will jeopardize your abstinence.

Your no also can be a reflection of your personal preferences. Lying to the boss about a colleague's whereabouts, slow-dancing with a highly intoxicated nightclub patron, or chaperoning a junior-high-school field trip may not be something you, as an individual with likes and dislikes, want to do. You have a right to say so—although it probably won't be easy. If you are like most compulsive eaters and bulimics, you've typically had as much trouble saying no to other people as you did saying no to food.

My recommendation is to start saying no in nonthreatening situations. Practice on people you'd find in your propriety circle. Say, "No, I'm not ready to order" to a waiter or "No, I'm not interested in aluminum siding" to the telephone solicitor. With people who are closer to you, practice on relatively minor issues. (Say, "No, dear. You'll have to keep looking for it yourself" when your child asks for help finding a misplaced toy.) Set "no" goals for yourself, making a commitment to say it—and mean it—a certain number of times per day or week.

For additional practice, ask a friend to role-play with you. Have that person make requests or overtures that usually are difficult for you to turn down. Encourage your friend to be pushy, manipulative, or guilt-inducing so that you can learn to say no to people who won't take no for an answer. This can be particularly helpful prior to an encounter with such a person or in preparation for an upcoming event where food may be pushed on you.

Set Limits on Boundary-Violating Behavior

Sometimes it takes more than a simple no to stop people from imposing upon you, invading your privacy, negating your needs, or making inappropriate demands. You should have no trouble spotting those boundary violations. They're the sorts of attitudes and actions that routinely ate away at you until you ate over them. You have a right to ask that they be discontinued. When you're ready to do that, take these steps:

1. Identify the behavior you'd like to see change and how you feel about it. Be specific—"Joe walks away while I'm in the middle of talking to him; it makes me feel ignored and unimportant," rather than "Joe never listens to me, and that ticks me off."

2. Think of an alternative to that behavior ("Joe could stay until I've finished my thought and then let me know he wants to end the conversation") or one that addresses your feelings ("Joe and I could set aside some time each week just to talk about what's on our minds").

3. Then present that information using this format:
   "I feel _(reaction)_
   when you _(behavior)_
   and would prefer that _(alternative)_."

   If you can define a *reasonable* consequence of continuing the old behavior rather than attempting the new (and are able to carry it out), you can add, "I realize this may be difficult for you, but it's important to me and if you won't, I'll need to (consequence)."

You'll feel more comfortable with this limit-setting technique if you write a script, role-play with a friend, or rehearse in front of a mirror. Try to sound as nonthreatening as possible and to convey your respect for the other person despite your unhappiness with his or her behavior.

Resolving Conflicts

A conflict is an emotionally charged collision of incompatible ideas, desires, or activities. It is the frustrating and often infuriating result of one person's efforts to get something he or she wants, thereby interfering with another person's ability to do the same. Although at the outset neither party is necessarily selfish or insensitive, each may seem that way to the other, a situation that can escalate into a full-scale battle of wills.

The ability to deal with conflicts and resolve them in a manner that allows all parties to come away with something they value is a skill that few people are taught. Indeed, most of us grew up in environments where exactly the opposite behavior was modeled for us. Consequently, when it comes to fighting fairly or ironing out disagreements of any kind, we are clueless. And because of the powerful emotions (anger, fear of rejection, resentment) often unleashed during interpersonal conflicts, we may have gone out of our way to avoid being directly involved in them.

Instead, we manipulated, caved in, accommodated, surreptitiously retaliated, or did nothing—and solved nothing. The same problems kept cropping up in our lives. The same buried rage and resentment kept threatening to rush to the surface, and we kept pushing it down again with the aid of food and addictive behavior.

The main source of our aversion to dealing directly with conflicts is the belief that doing so can only lead to pain, loss of control, words or actions we'll later regret, and quite possibly the demise of entire relationships. Although we can support this perception by pointing to our own and other people's past experiences, all conflicts are not bitter, no-holds-barred confrontations that end marriages, friendships, or employment. Most are merely disagreements that will end with improved understanding, solved problems, mutual satisfaction, and strengthened relationships. The key is to fight fairly and choose your fights carefully.

Before Doing Anything, Locate the Source of Conflict

Try to get a sense of the underlying needs or emotions that may be triggering both the other person's actions and your own desire to run, scream, or give that person a piece of your mind. Are you at odds with your boss over facts (for example, whether or not your sales were slipping) or the boss's presentation of those facts (chewing you out in front of the entire staff)? Is it your spouse's objective (to get you to help hang pictures when you want to watch TV) or your spouse's method (coming into the TV room and pounding nails for the pictures into the wall above your head) that has you thinking about strangling your mate?

In addition, when disagreeing with a parent or someone who reminds you of that parent, check to make sure that old business—unresolved conflicts from the past—isn't instigating an overreaction.

Merely stopping to consider these points gives you time to cool off and think more objectively about your situation. Any answers you come up with will help you choose a more appropriate and beneficial course of action.

Sometimes you'll discover that what looked like the makings of a major blowout was actually a misunderstanding on your part. Or you'll recognize that you basically agree with the other person's position and that his or her obnoxious delivery, although irritating, doesn't matter to you enough to get into a fight over it. You can *let go and move on*. In other instances, it will quickly become apparent that the other person isn't going to give an inch and that your best bet will be to *accept that and work on not allowing it to rob you of your self-respect or peace of mind*.

More often than you might imagine, however, you'll be able to spot some common ground, some small point of agreement, shared feeling, or even mutual confusion that can serve as the starting point for discussion and negotiation. Here are seven guidelines to improve the odds that those discussions will lead to constructively settled conflicts rather than destructively repetitive or escalating ones. Although this process won't always work out fairly, over the long haul, things tend to even themselves out.

1. *Keep your ego—the part of you that wants to be right no matter what—in check.* Your goal is to foster communication about

the area of conflict and ultimately negotiate an agreement that allows both of you to get at least some of what you want. That won't happen if you enter into the discussion intent on saving face, getting the other person to back down and admit he or she was wrong, or keeping score. If such ideas should cross your mind—and trust me, they will—ask yourself: "Would I rather be right or be happy?" Hopefully, the choice will be clear.

2. *Watch your timing.* Don't try to resolve conflicts when the other person is in an inappropriate frame of mind, on the way out the door, or trying to concentrate on something else. I also recommend waiting until *your* emotions are not running so high that you might lose your temper, burst into tears, start shaking, or forget the point you were making.

   Of course, you won't always have the luxury of choosing the time to discuss your concerns—especially when the other person makes that choice for you by insisting that you "work this out right here, right now." You'll have to make do under those circumstances, perhaps by excusing yourself for a moment. Staying put and taking several slow, calming breaths helps too.

3. *Listen closely and compassionately.* Yes, that's tough to do when the discussion is emotionally charged and there's a chance that you'll have to give up something you want or get something you don't. However, it's definitely worth the effort. Purposely train your attention on what the other person is conveying both verbally and nonverbally. Try to "hear" the feelings as well as the words. Before going on to your own thoughts and feelings, *summarize* what you heard. *Verify* that it was what the other person meant. It may not be. Many things, including your distaste for conflict, can lead to misinterpretations.

   Ask for *clarification.* If you're confused, say so. If something seems to be missing, mention it. The more information you can obtain—even if it's painful to hear—the more you'll have to work with when you're both ready to move into a problem-solving mode.

At the same time, realize that the other person may not be as reasonable about all this as you are. Be receptive, but somewhat detached. When the other person attempts to push your buttons, try to step back and process information as if you were watching someone else playing your part in the discussion.

4. *Look for points of agreement.* Somewhere in that tirade lies a grain of truth, something that you can appreciate or relate to—even if you think it's illogical or unfair. Grab hold of it and start your response there. You might say, "I can see how you'd feel that way" and share an experience that had a similar effect on you. Or try, "You know, you could be right about . . ." and, after noting that possibility, gently steer the conversation toward the point of contention you'd like to address.

5. *Be honest—but choose your words carefully.* Sure, you may want to berate the other person up and down and list every insensitive thing he or she has ever done to you. But what will that accomplish? Remember your goal, keep your cool, and speak in a tone that won't escalate the argument. Talk about what *you* see, hear, feel, and need rather than what *the other person* did that was wrong, insensitive, and so on. Avoid inflammatory words—globalizations such as *always* and *never* and derogatory labels. Don't rub in weaknesses or call someone else's feelings stupid.

Trying too hard to avoid upsetting the other person or rushing to apologize for "making" someone feel bad as soon as he or she shows signs of becoming upset isn't particularly helpful either. It gets you off track and leaves you wide open to manipulation.

6. *If things get too hot, take time-outs to cool off.* Again, conversations aimed at resolving conflicts do not have to be intense, angry confrontations. They won't be if you inject a little humor when you can. Try a touch now and then or some

silence. Take a break or a moment to share your feelings about the conversation and the commendable effort both of you are putting into it. Even in the heat of battle, it's possible to show respect to your opponents.

7. *Negotiate*. First, *define the issue*. What's really at stake here? What is the problem you are hoping to solve? What do you need from each other or the situation? While sometimes clear-cut, even what the conflict is about may be perceived differently by each party. Talk about it.

Next, *propose possible solutions, discuss the rewards and costs of each, and select one*. Chances are that both of you will come to the bargaining table with the solution you prefer in hand. Think of other alternatives. Tinker with your original propositions. Weigh the costs and benefits of each possibility. Look for win-win outcomes—ones that allow both of you to get something you need without costing either of you more than you're willing to pay. And choose a course of action that both of you can live with for now.

Then, *set a time frame*. Rather than looking at your negotiated agreement as the final solution to your problem, think of it as an experiment. This not only takes the sting out of some of the compromising you may have to do, but it also gives you an out if your solution proves to be unworkable. Agree to abide by your mutual decision for a specific period of time. When that time elapses, evaluate your decision and *renegotiate, if necessary*.

PART IV

THE JOURNEY CONTINUES

CHAPTER THIRTEEN

One Last Pitfall:
Getting Hooked on Recovery

"I don't understand it," Marcia said. "I've been eating the same way and maintaining the same weight for almost three years, but for the past few weeks, I've been really worried. I keep thinking that I'm going to gain weight and checking to make sure I haven't. Yesterday, I got on the scale four times. And I'm constantly asking my husband and kids if I look heavier. They keep telling me I don't, but I won't believe them."

If there was even a remote possibility that Marcia might have to miss her aerobics class, she became irritable. And even though she had dined in restaurants throughout her recovery, it took her forever to make a selection from a menu. "I'll find something I can have and want to have," she explained, "but when the waitress gets to me, I order something else, something that I don't really care for but I think I should eat because it has fewer calories."

Fearing that her renewed preoccupation with food and weight was a warning that she was about to relapse, Marcia increased the number of OA meetings she attended and began soliciting advice from fellow recovering food addicts. After being consulted three times in as many days, one of them posed a question that initially left Marcia perplexed.

"What's going on in your life?" this longtime friend asked.

"I just *told* you" was Marcia's exasperated reply. "I'm obsessing about food and on the verge of losing my abstinence."

"I mean, what *else* is going on?" her friend countered. "How are things at work, at home, with your kids? What's *really* bothering you?"

Quite a bit, it turned out. Layoff rumors were running rampant at the advertising agency where Marcia worked, and as one of the most recently hired employees, she was sure she would be among the first to be pink-slipped. Her daughter hadn't made the cheerleading squad and seemed inconsolable. And her mom thought her dad might have started drinking again. There was nothing she could do about those problems, Marcia commented, "except worry myself sick."

"Or create an imaginary problem you *can* do something about," her friend added, and a light bulb blinked on in Marcia's head. In one of those flashes of insight that all of us have now and then, she not only realized what she'd been doing for the past few weeks, but also recognized a pattern that had been repeating itself throughout her recovery.

"Almost every time areas of my life that had nothing to do with food or weight were less than perfect, I'd start to obsess about food and weight," Marcia noted. Assuming that she was about to relapse, she would begin working her program more feverishly, tinkering with her food plan, thinking about almost nothing but her recovery. In essence, she was using her recovery program the same way she had once used food and dieting—to feel as if she had some control over her life, to relieve her anxiety, and to alter her mood.

Marcia's experience is far from unique. Each and every one of us gravitates to the familiar. And what's familiar to those of us who became addicted to a substance or activity and struggled to gain some semblance of control over an unmanageable life is addictive behavior and struggling. Consequently, we can turn anything into something to be obsessive or compulsive about—including abstinence and recovery. Instead of *employing* the tools of recovery to free ourselves from dependency on external sources of self-worth, accept ourselves as we are, and learn to deal effectively with life's ups and downs, we become dependent on them to supply us with a sense of security and control, to make us feel good about ourselves, and to avoid facing various realities of everyday life.

The difference is subtle, but significant. You can see it by checking your vision of wellness and asking yourself: "Is my current approach to recovery moving me closer to that state of physical, emotional, and spiritual health or keeping it beyond my grasp?" Also, look for the following signs.

Symptoms of "Recovery Addiction"
Living by Rigid Rules
Those of us who get hooked on our recovery programs set up a system of hard-and-fast rules for our recovery and, thinking that we must follow them to the letter at all times and under all circumstances, may go so far as to eat the same foods on the same day each week or panic whenever something we planned to eat is unavailable.

We may establish recovery rituals and become downright superstitious about them. We act as if having our meals at specific times, praying for a minimum of ten minutes every morning, writing in our journals, or repeating certain affirmations daily could make or break our recovery, and we become quite upset when anyone or anything interferes with those activities.

Feeling Lots of Guilt and Self-Doubt
Although it's natural to feel unsure of ourselves when embarking on a new way of life, those of us who are prone to developing a dependency on our recovery program never really stop wondering if we are working our program correctly or well enough. We question the "rightness" of our food plans and our use of other recovery tools, even though they're effective and comfortable—or maybe *because* they're comfortable.

This is getting too easy, we think. *Things are going too well. Could I be fooling myself? Am I in denial again?* To make sure we aren't, we begin tinkering with our food plans or placing new, more stringent restrictions on our behavior.

Allowing Fear of Jeopardizing Our Abstinence to Override Other Considerations

We seem to think of our recovery as far too fragile to withstand even the slightest temptations and go out of our way to avoid them, sometimes to the point of sacrificing our other needs and interests. I've heard recovering clients and friends tell me that they'd decided not to attend a banquet where they were to receive a well-deserved award because dinner would have been served two hours later than their usual mealtime or that they'd chosen a camping vacation over a dream cruise because the former allowed them to prepare their own meals. One woman I know even stood outside in subzero temperatures for more than an hour while her car was being repaired because she was afraid that the aroma of food coming from a roadside cafeteria would compel her to eat something that wasn't on her food plan.

Continuing to Avoid People, Places, and Things That Once Triggered Addictive Behavior for Months or Years After Becoming Abstinent

This includes never eating in a restaurant, turning down all invitations to social functions where food will be served buffet-style, refusing to attend family gatherings, and eating alone in our offices so we won't see or smell our co-workers' food.

Using Recovery-Oriented Activities to Avoid Anxiety-Provoking Situations

Attending OA meetings, going to workshops or seminars, reading recovery literature, spending less time with slippery people or in slippery places, and working on ourselves in therapy are all worthy endeavors. But they can also become excuses not to venture out or take risks in other areas of our lives.

Telling our best friend that we can't go to a singles dance because we must attend an OA meeting that evening, even though we could easily go to a different meeting, or turning down an invitation to speak at a conference because it would require us to be out of town on the day we usually see our therapist, who could reschedule us, are two examples of this symptom of recovery addiction.

Worrying About Weight Gain When Our Routine Has Not Changed

As it was for Marcia, this almost always indicates that something unrelated to our body size is bothering us and that we have unwittingly converted our feelings about that circumstance into a renewed and frequently obsessive concern about our recovery.

Getting Sloppy

An example of this is slightly but repeatedly increasing our food intake when we are under stress and then putting the rest of our lives on hold while we "clean up" our abstinence and rededicate ourselves to our recovery.

Sounding Like a Broken Record at OA or Therapy Group Meetings

Many compulsive eaters and bulimics reach a certain point in their recovery and then get stuck. They become abstinent, uncover a few possible explanations for their eating disorders, complete a Fourth Step inventory, and then, out of fear or the belief that they've done all there is to do, switch their focus from changing and growing to merely hanging on to the progress they've already made. If you find yourself repeating the same old platitudes, talking almost exclusively about realizations that you came to months or even years ago, or sharing experiences that you think others can benefit from but rarely discussing anything that's actually bothering you, chances are that you're stuck too.

Sponsoring More OA Newcomers Than We Can Handle

This allows us to become absorbed by other people's recovery as well as our own; it also leaves us with even less time or energy to face new challenges or pursue new interests that might prove to be more than we could handle.

Remaining Hypervigilant and Looking for Signs of a Relapse
We become overly conscious that our disease is behind every door, waiting to pounce on us and doing one-handed push-ups so that it will be strong enough to overpower us.

Although many of the foregoing behaviors may have been reasonable and necessary when our abstinence was new and unfamiliar, continuing to focus our attention on recovery to the exclusion of almost everything else is not only unnecessary over the long haul, but also unhealthy. When I say this, I am not arguing against ongoing involvement in a program of recovery. I'm arguing for flexibility and balance. That is, after all, what the good life is all about.

What's Going On and What to Do About It

Why do we develop unhealthy dependencies on our recovery program? More often than not, we get hooked because *we're experiencing conflicts or confusion in other areas of our lives that we'd rather not face.* Our rules and rituals and single-minded devotion to recovery offer us the same sort of smoke screen that compulsive eating, obsessive dieting, or bingeing and purging once did. Our lives appear to be more manageable, but in reality, we are still floundering and missing out on many sources of satisfaction.

So the next time you catch yourself behaving in the manner I just described, do a spot check to see how things are going at work, at home, with your family members, or in other relationships. Ask yourself if you've been under a lot of pressure lately, experienced a loss or change of status, or begun grappling with the issues of midlife. Have particularly painful issues been rising to the surface in therapy, or have pleasant surprises—experiences that were beyond your grasp while you were into the food—been coming your way?

Once you've recognized what's going on behind the smoke screen, muster up your courage and deal with it. Use the applicable self-help strategies found in earlier sections of this book, or turn to other resources—therapy, literature, workshops, continuing education courses—that address those specific issues and *not* just addiction or recovery.

We also get hooked on recovery programs when *our primary motivation for being and staying in one is sheer terror:* when we can't stop thinking about the way we used to be or worrying about returning to that dismal and depressing state. Instead of pursuing health and happiness, we're running from addiction and being controlled by our fear of relapse. We seem to believe that it's better to live limited lives revolving solely around recovery than to risk giving up a single ritual that we're convinced was responsible for saving us from food addiction.

We seem to think that if we ate tuna instead of chicken on Thursday, skipped an OA meeting, didn't read from five meditation books first thing in the morning, or allowed ourselves to be within fifty paces of a buffet table, the entire foundation on which our abstinence is built would crumble. And therein lies the crux of the problem.

We see our recovery as a house of cards tenuously balanced on a rickety card table and subject to demolition by the slightest breeze. What's more, we believe that we single-handedly erected that structure by taking specific actions that we must repeat again and again for all eternity. We haven't accepted that we are in recovery because we went through a process that changed us or that those changes can last.

To release the death grip our fear of relapse has on us and to graciously accept the gifts true recovery offers us, we need to do the following:

- *Update our self-image.* Look at all the ways that you are different than you were when you first embarked on your recovery program, and revise your Fourth Step inventory or list of pluses and minuses to reflect those changes. Identify strengths that you've developed and difficulties you've overcome. Note how your body, your outlook, your energy level, and your relationships have improved. These aren't illusions, but they may feel as if they are, because your internal image of yourself hasn't caught up with external reality yet. Give it a little push by turning any evidence of growth that you uncover into positive affirmations:

- "I am kind, compassionate, and honest with myself."
- "I have a new way of eating and relating to food."
- "Abstinence comes to me easily and effortlessly."
- "I'm better than I've ever been and getting better all the time."
- "I accept the miracle of recovery and trust it to continue."

- *Look at the broader picture.* It was not the specific actions we took, but rather the overall process we got involved in that enabled us to overcome our eating disorders. An integral part of that process was admitting our own powerlessness to control our eating or manage our lives and allowing a power greater than ourselves to help us do what we could not do alone. We negate that essential premise when we act as if eating at eight, noon, and six and weighing every portion we consumed made us abstinent or as if meditating for twenty minutes every single day, having a particular sponsor, and calling him or her every morning brought about our recovery. We are trying to control our recovery by religiously adhering to the rules and rituals we established for ourselves—and it won't work.

The pressure we're placing on ourselves will backfire sooner or later. We'll rebel against those rigid restrictions and lose the very thing we're fighting so hard to maintain.

So loosen your grip and reacknowledge your powerlessness. Work less on your physical recovery and more on the spiritual aspect of your program. Reexamine your beliefs and revise them as needed.

Picture your fears and limitations floating away in the basket of a hot air balloon or on the wings of an angel, and imagine yourself surrounded by a protective white light. Then let faith in a Higher Power play a greater role in your life. You'll find everything you need, including recovery, coming to you with far less exertion and far more serenity.

A third reason for getting hooked on recovery programs is *the absence of other meaningful and satisfying activities or relationships.* We may have replaced our compulsive behaviors with recovery-related endeavors and looked no further. As a result, those endeavors and contact with other recovering men and women became the only sources of gratification in our lives. To reduce our dependency, we must expand our horizons.

Grab the wellness wheel you created way back in chapter 7 and get busy. Visualize the life you want. Bolster your confidence with positive affirmations. Set goals and pursue them one step at a time, rewarding yourself for every ounce of progress. Then make room in your life for wellness and time for new activities by slowly relinquishing some of your rituals. Attend one less meeting a week. Sponsor fewer newcomers. Read recovery literature or meditate only when you want to or feel it could help you through a rough moment instead of doing it for a predetermined length of time every single day. Your abstinence won't disappear into thin air.

Relinquish some control as well. Try adding variety to your food plan or making decisions based on wants or needs other than protecting your abstinence. If the option you choose will put you in a situation that poses a real threat to your abstinence, simply figure out how you can reduce that threat without avoiding the situation entirely.

If you hear yourself saying that you can't do something because it conflicts with a recovery-related activity, make sure you don't mean that you'd rather not do it because you're nervous or lack confidence in your ability to succeed at it. If that's the case—and quite often it is—take steps similar to those described earlier in this book in order to manage your anxiety, conquer your fear, or boost your self-esteem.

CHAPTER FOURTEEN

The Final Phase:
Undependence

Before I began working on this book, I conducted an informal poll of people in recovery for five years or longer who seemed to have adjusted fully to their new way of life. I asked them what had changed for them since they first embarked on their recovery programs. This is what three of those men and women told me.

"I'm much more relaxed," Debra declared, "less afraid of relapse—or anything, really. Instead of fighting my compulsions, I trust my recovery. Instead of trying to control and maneuver everything, I just make sure to do the things I can and leave the rest to a Higher Power. And instead of always thinking about how bad I used to be, I focus on how much better I am and how much better I want to be. I have faith that things will work out the way they're supposed to—even if they don't work out exactly the way I want them to."

"I used to wake up every morning and go through this whole list of promises to myself," Arlene recalled. "I'd promise to be abstinent, not to let little things get to me, to handle whatever happened to me without eating over it, and on and on. I had to recommit myself to every detail of abstinent living every single day and then watch myself like a hawk to make sure I didn't slip up anywhere. Now I just get up, go out, and live. I know what I have to do to stay in recovery, and I do it. That's that."

Ron, a radio soundman who tipped the scales at 360 pounds before getting into recovery nine years ago, considers himself reborn. "I used to think of myself as a great big nothing," he said.

"Now I look at myself and see someone with courage, ingenuity, friends, talents, inherent goodness. I have the confidence to try new things, and even if I fall flat on my face, I give myself credit for trying. Then I pick myself up and try something else. I've had more success by trying and sometimes failing than I ever did when I wouldn't try because I thought I'd fail."

Debra's, Arlene's, and Ron's words capture the essence of *undependence*—a term I use to describe the new and decidedly different approach to life and sobriety that emerges in the third phase of recovery.

Undependence is an attitude of . . . optimism . . . self-confidence . . . hope . . . and pride in the things we've accomplished thus far. Freed from the despair of food addiction and the desperation that often accompanies physical recovery, we discover more personal strengths and become more willing to face life without mood-altering substances or activities, including those related to our recovery. We learn to walk crutchless. Instead of relying almost entirely on people, places, and things outside ourselves to supply us with a sense of adequacy and acceptance, we begin to accept ourselves, blemishes and all, and feel worthwhile regardless of external circumstances.

Undependence is also a life-style—one that supports growth, happiness, sanity, and action. We do less soul-searching and data-gathering than we did in the emotional, social, and spiritual phase of our recovery and make more conscious, conscientious choices. Our lives are not free of pain or trouble, of course. Whose are? However, with the fog of addiction and denial lifted, we can view problems more realistically and work through them more quickly when they do arise.

Although the outcomes may be less than perfect, they'll certainly be better than the ones we ended up with when we automatically reacted to stressful situations by engaging in compulsive behavior. By the time we reach this stage of recovery, we hardly ever do that anymore. The negative cycle we were trapped in for so many years has been broken, and a new, self-perpetuating positive growth pattern is taking root and flourishing.

The primary task of the third phase of recovery is to live our lives fully and free of unhealthy dependencies. Our entrance into this phase is marked by an internal shift, an attitude change that tends to be subtle rather than cathartic. There's no fanfare. No fireworks. No epiphany or therapeutic breakthrough. We simply notice that we've stopped struggling. Everything about abstinence and daily living seems easier, more natural, as if we'd been behaving the same way all our lives. We no longer doubt that we are in recovery or worry that our newfound sense of physical, emotional, and spiritual well-being is an illusion that will evaporate one night while we are sleeping. We know in our hearts and souls that we won't be going back to the way we used to be, that our old behavior just isn't an option for us anymore.

If your recovery is still relatively new and unsettling or a seemingly endless uphill battle, it may be difficult for you to imagine yourself ever sharing that point of view. But you can, and if you stick with your recovery program, toughing out the rough times and working it even when that's the last thing you feel like doing, you will. In fact, whether you know it and are consciously trying to or not, you're moving toward undependence at this very moment.

The personal transformation that occurs as we enter phase three is a natural by-product of the process we set in motion when we admitted we were powerless over our eating disorders and needed help to overcome them. Each day of freedom from compulsive eating or bingeing and purging, each task of physical recovery, every healthy relationship we develop, whittles away at our old thinking and offers us new ideas that add up to an undependent outlook.

At some point—and that point is different for everyone—our attitudinal building blocks fall into place, and we experience what a recovering bulimic colleague of mine compares to tiles in a mosaic rearranging themselves in a new pattern. I think of it as jigsaw puzzle pieces finally fitting together to form a coherent picture, one that incorporates the following six interwoven themes:

Acceptance

Although I lost all the weight I needed to lose during my first postrelapse year of abstaining from compulsive eating, neither my new body size nor my new life-style—which I've maintained to this day—seemed real to me back then. I was working a solid recovery program but couldn't bring myself to say that I was a *recovering* compulsive eater.

I ran three miles a day five days a week, but I didn't think of myself as a runner. I wore normal-, sometimes single-digit-sized clothing, but while shopping, I routinely reached for items that were several sizes too large for me. In my mind, I was still a fat, miserable, out-of-control food addict who wore extra-large peasant dresses and got winded climbing one flight of stairs.

Sometimes I'd catch a glimpse of myself in a mirror or storefront window and actually feel surprised. "Who is that person?" I'd ask myself jokingly. But I seriously thought of that slender woman's reflection as belonging to someone else, someone I dared not get used to having around.

That perception probably sounds familiar, since years of dieting failure taught those of us with eating disorders to think of any weight loss as temporary. Our new, slimmer bodies were only on loan to us. We would enjoy them for a while, but sooner or later, we'd get our old bodies back. Most of us brought that attitude with us into recovery and extended it to every aspect of overcoming our eating disorders.

Convinced that it was only a matter of time until we'd fail, we didn't trust our success. We were sure we'd wake up one morning and discover that our new way of life had been a dream, that nothing had really changed, or that all of our progress had vanished. It took more than three years of abstinent living to convince me to think otherwise.

Unlike most of my other attitude changes, I can recall the exact moment when I decided to stop waiting for the other shoe to drop. Again, I had caught a glimpse of myself in my bedroom mirror. Only this time I smiled at the woman I saw there and said to her, "You know, I like you. I think I'll keep you."

Then, laughing at how crazy I was to be talking to my reflection in the first place, I started going through my drawers and closets, pulling out my fat clothes—even the ones that were only a size or two larger than my thin wardrobe and reserved for minor five- to ten-pound weight gains. I gave everything to a homeless shelter. I also threw out all the calorie- and carbohydrate-counting and diet books that I'd kept just in case I ever again needed to drop a few pounds quickly.

I began to see the world with new eyes then too. I took compliments more gracefully. I was more receptive to friendly overtures and became friendlier myself. I abstained from compulsive eating, not because I was afraid of what might happen if I didn't, but because it came as naturally to me as breathing. It was part of the new life I had worked hard to create and had at long last accepted was mine for keeps.

Accepting that the person you've become is who you really are and that the gifts of recovery are real and lasting are the cornerstones of an undependent attitude. They allow you to stop worrying about losing the benefits you've gained and start learning to live with them, to trust that you truly are *in recovery* and, with ease and confidence, to act accordingly.

Commitment

A commitment is a pledge or promise without an escape clause, a decision we make once and have no intention of reconsidering or revoking at a later date. Whenever we're in doubt, we remember our commitment and honor it. We do what we had previously pledged to do.

In early recovery, we made daily commitments. Each time we wrote down a food plan and reported it to an OA sponsor, other knowledgeable individual, or a Higher Power, we were committing ourselves to be abstinent—for that day. For the next twenty-four hours, we pledged, eating certain foods, overeating, or bingeing and purging would not be options for us.

Since commitment had never been our strong suit, at first we may have weaseled our way out of even these one-day-at-a-time promises. But eventually we managed to keep our promise for twenty-four hours, then forty-eight, seventy-two, a week, and longer. We stopped looking for reasons not to keep it, ways to get around it, or circumstances in which breaking our promise to be abstinent was understandable, if not completely justifiable.

Over time, honoring our commitment became a habit. It became easier to resist temptation, to attend functions where taboo foods would be served, to walk past the office break room without even thinking about the box of doughnuts sitting next to the coffee machine. "This morning I made a commitment to be abstinent," we reminded ourselves, "and so I will be."

In the undependent living stage, we take that premise and extend it to recovery as a whole. *We commit ourselves to a new way of life* and, by doing so, eliminate the option of returning to our old ways at all. Arlene was referring to this sort of commitment when she said, "I know what I have to do to stay in recovery, and I do it. That's that."

In this day and age of seemingly endless options and possibilities, many of us shy away from fully committing ourselves to anything. We don't want to be pinned down or have our freedom of choice limited in any way. Well, a commitment to recovery will prevent us from doing whatever we feel like doing whenever we feel like doing it.

But a commitment to recovery also liberates us. It frees us from having to constantly agonize over whether or not we will be abstinent today, be honest with ourselves in this situation, or do what is necessary for our continued recovery at any given moment. We've already made that choice. We no longer have to worry about that aspect of our lives. It is taken care of. And we can stop looking over our shoulder to see if our eating disorder is gaining on us. Even if we should slip, with our commitment to guide us we can get back on track immediately and keep moving forward.

Faith

The fundamental, unshakable belief in a force that is more universal, powerful, and benevolent than our own egos is essential to long-term recovery. In whatever way we define and feel comfortable with it, our relationship with a Higher Power gives us a sense of wholeness and satisfaction.

The spiritual element of recovery offers us the serenity and quiet self-assurance that come from living in harmony with our own values and the world around us. It provides us with opportunities to be still and listen—to our instincts, our feelings, our inner wisdom. And it enables us to relax, let go of our emotional attachment to certain outcomes, and, as Debra put it, to have "faith that things will work out the way they're supposed to, even if they don't work out exactly the way we want them to."

Without faith, we put ourselves in charge. We devise elaborate schemes detailing when and how people should do things, and we become upset when they don't. We assume responsibility for situations we actually have no control over and feel compelled to worry about and manipulate circumstances or people so that our expectations will be met or the consequences we fear will be avoided. This *always* got us into trouble in the past.

Faith is an antidote for fear, indecision, and overcontrol. When we believe in and rely on a Higher Power to help us over life's rough spots, we can

- concentrate on doing the best we can in the areas that are within our control and leave the rest alone
- cope with situations that are beyond our control without being overwhelmed by them
- face our fears rather than being paralyzed by them
- take risks without being unduly anxious ahead of time or unduly upset if our ventures don't succeed

If you still aren't sure that you have the sort of faith or relationship with a Higher Power that I've been describing, continue acting as if you do. It may sound odd or hypocritical, but it works. By going through the motions of asking a Higher Power for help, letting go of control, and being receptive to miracles, you reap many of the same benefits and usually discover that somewhere along the line, you managed to develop real faith.

Self-Esteem

Gone are the days of feeling inferior, of measuring our worth by numbers on a scale or other people's approval, and of having our confidence rise and fall depending on how fat or thin we feel. Our experiences in recovery make it possible for us to recognize our strengths as well as our weaknesses and show us numerous aspects of ourselves that are unique, valuable, and ours to keep regardless of what is going on around us.

As our recovery progresses, we realize that we are more than our mirror image, more than our eating problems, and more than recovering compulsive eaters or bulimics. We have dreams and goals, talents and flaws, that have nothing to do with our eating disorders or recovery program. They are simply additional facets of our identity, new shades in our increasingly detailed and colorful self-portrait. Some we like more than others, but none can stir up the sense of shame and inferiority that used to be our constant companions. Now that we've traded self-criticism and self-loathing for self-acceptance and self-love, we feel worthy of the nice things that happen to us and confident about our ability to be joyful, productive, sociable, and at peace.

Just as our lack of self-esteem contributed to the development of our eating disorders, our newfound, internal sense of self-worth will supply us with the courage, security, and motivation to keep progressing in recovery—and life.

Looking Forward to the Future

During the first two stages of recovery, we walked into the future backward. Although we were making progress, our attention was focused on the past. We needed to keep the memory of where we had been fresh in our minds so that we could learn where not to go and what not to do. In phase three, we turn around. We don't forget the past. We just stop dwelling on it or using our fear of returning to it as our primary motivation for being in recovery. We focus instead on where we are now and where we hope to be in the future. Our eyes open to the myriad possibilities and people around us. We embrace life and are primed to make the most of it.

Realizing that our needs are not the same as they were during our childhood, our years of food addiction, or earlier in our recovery, we begin to ask ourselves, *What do I need now? What is really important to the person I've become and am becoming? How can I create a life that is truly full and fulfilling for me?* We use the answers we generate to refine the vision of physical, emotional, and spiritual wellness we developed previously. Then, encouraged by the success we've already experienced, we get down to the business of turning that vision into a reality.

Empowerment

Throughout our lives, we used substances and activities to help us cope with situations we felt powerless to change. But once the veil of addiction is lifted, we frequently see that some of those situations were amenable to change and that there were things we could have done to improve them. Recovery gives us increased awareness, more choices, and greater willingness to assume responsibility for our actions. With those gains comes the recognition that we can

- say no with our voices instead of building a wall of fat to ward off sexual predators
- resolve marital conflicts constructively instead of eating over our rocky marriages
- be active rather than reactive, setting and pursuing reasonable goals instead of sitting around waiting for things to happen
- quiet the inner voice that whines, "I want what I want when I want it," and postpone gratification while we consider a variety of alternatives and make choices that are in the best interest of everyone involved

As a result, we feel, perhaps for the first time in our lives, a sense of empowerment. We realize that we can have a positive impact on the world around us and operate in that world feeling strong and effective. And we can do that without incessantly, and for the most part futilely, trying to control other people's thoughts, feelings, and actions.

Drawing upon our newfound sense of personal power and our ever-growing repertoire of coping skills and problem-solving strategies, we can effectively deal with and positively change the circumstances we once used our eating disorders to escape. And we can change ourselves as well, becoming healthier, happier, more adaptable, more compassionate, and more confident with each passing day.

Acceptance, commitment, faith, self-esteem, looking forward to the future, and empowerment are the tiles in all of our undependence mosaics, but how and when they fall into place is a highly individual matter. The transformation cannot be rushed, willed to happen, or objectively measured. There are no step-by-step instructions for achieving it and no stages after it. As you may have figured out by now, undependence is more than a stage of recovery. It's a physically, emotionally, and spiritually well way of life. The only alternative to it is to become dependent again, and regrettably, that will happen to some of us—but not necessarily for long. Having gotten a taste of freedom from compulsive overeating or bulimia and the true sense of peace and fulfillment that accompanies it, you'll be highly motivated to return for more.

The Twelve Steps Of
Alcoholics Anonymous*

1. We admitted we were powerless over alcohol—that our lives had become unmanageable.

2. Came to believe that a Power greater than ourselves could restore us to sanity.

3. Made a decision to turn our will and our lives over to the care of God *as we understood Him.*

4. Made a searching and fearless moral inventory of ourselves.

5. Admitted to God, to ourselves, and to another human being the exact nature of our wrongs.

6. Were entirely ready to have God remove all these defects of character.

7. Humbly asked Him to remove our shortcomings.

8. Made a list of all persons we had harmed, and became willing to make amends to them all.

9. Made direct amends to such people wherever possible, except when to do so would injure them or others.

10. Continued to take personal inventory and when we were wrong promptly admitted it.

11. Sought through prayer and meditation to improve our conscious contact with God *as we understood Him,* praying only for knowledge of His will for us and the power to carry that out.

12. Having had a spiritual awakening as the result of these steps, we tried to carry this message to alcoholics, and to practice these principles in all our affairs.

---

*The Twelve Steps of A.A. are taken from *Alcoholics Anonymous*, 3d ed., published by A.A. World Services, Inc., New York, N.Y., 59-60. Reprinted with permission of A.A. World Services, Inc. (See editor's note on copyright page.)

The Twelve Steps Of
Overeaters Anonymous*

1. We admitted we were powerless over food—that our lives had become unmanageable.
2. Came to believe that a Power greater than ourselves could restore us to sanity.
3. Made a decision to turn our will and our lives over to the care of God *as we understood Him*.
4. Made a searching and fearless moral inventory of ourselves.
5. Admitted to God, to ourselves, and to another human being the exact nature of our wrongs.
6. Were entirely ready to have God remove all these defects of character.
7. Humbly asked Him to remove our shortcomings.
8. Made a list of all persons we had harmed, and became willing to make amends to them all.
9. Made direct amends to such people wherever possible, except when to do so would injure them or others.
10. Continued to take personal inventory and when we were wrong, promptly admitted it.
11. Sought through prayer and meditation to improve our conscious contact with God *as we understood Him*, praying only for knowledge of His will for us and the power to carry that out.
12. Having had a spiritual awakening as the result of these steps, we tried to carry this message to compulsive overeaters and to practice these principles in all our affairs.

*Permission to use the Twelve Steps of Alcoholics Anonymous for adaptation granted to Overeaters Anonymous by AA World Services, Inc. The Twelve Steps of Overeaters Anonymous, as adapted, are reprinted here with the permission of Overeaters Anonymous, Inc. (See editor's note on copyright page.)

Suggested Reading

W isdom, according to Winston Churchill, is knowing what to do; talent is knowing how to do it; and virtue is doing it. Undependence is a combination of all three, and the more you can learn about dealing with your emotions, other people, and potentially troublesome situations, the more undependent you'll be. Here are some resources to help you do that.

Overcoming Eating Disorders

Cauwells, Janice M. *Bulimia: The Binge-Purge Compulsion.* New York: Doubleday, 1983.

Greeson, Janet. *It's Not What You're Eating, It's What's Eating You.* New York: Pocket Books, 1990.

Hollis, Judi, Ph.D. *Fat Is a Family Affair.* Center City, Minn.: Hazelden Educational Materials, 1985.

————. *Resisting Recovery.* Center City, Minn.: Hazelden Educational Materials, 1985.

Rogers, Ronald L., and Chandler Scott McMillin. *Relapse Traps: How to Avoid the Twelve Most Common Pitfalls in Recovery.* New York: Bantam, 1992.

Sheppard, Kay. *Food Addiction: The Body Knows.* Deerfield Beach, Fla.: Health Communications, 1989.

Sundermeyer, Colleen A., Ph.D. *Emotional Weight: Are You Overweight in Mind or Body?* Ann Arbor, Mich.: New Outlook, 1989.

Waldrop, Heidi. *Showing Up for Life: A Recovering Overeater's Triumph over Compulsion.* New York: Ballantine, 1991.

Related Problems

Alcoholics Anonymous [also called "The Big Book"]. New York: AA World Services, Inc., 1976.

Beattie, Melody. *Codependent No More: How to Stop Controlling Others and Start Taking Care of Yourself.* New York/San Francisco: HarperCollins, 1987.

Covington, Stephanie, Ph.D. *Awakening Your Sexuality: A Recovery Guide for Women.* San Francisco: HarperSanFrancisco, 1991.

Covington, Stephanie, and Liana Beckett. *The Enchanted Forest: The Path from Relationship Addiction.* New York: HarperCollins, 1988.

Elliot, Miriam, Ph.D., and Susan Meltsner, MSW. *The Perfectionist's Predicament.* New York: Wm. Morrow, 1991.

Kasl, Charlotte Davis. *Women, Sex, and Addiction: A Search for Love and Power.* New York: Ticknor & Fields, 1989.

Leman, Kevin. *The Pleasers: Women Who Can't Say No and the Men Who Control Them.* Tarrytown, N.Y.: Dell, 1992.

Norwood, Robin. *Women Who Love Too Much: When You Keep Wishing and Hoping He'll Change.* Los Angeles: J. P. Tarcher, 1985.

Weiss, Laurie. *Recovery from Co-Dependency.* Deerfield Beach, Fla.: Health Communications, 1989.

Why Me?

Becker, Robert A. *Don't Talk, Don't Trust, Don't Feel: Our Family Dysfunction Secrets.* Deerfield Beach, Fla.: Health Communications, 1991.

Black, Claudia. *Double Duty: Sexually Abused.* Denver, Col.: MAC Publishing, 1990.

Halvorson, Ronald S., and Valerie B. Deilgat, eds. *The Twelve Steps—A Way Out: A Working Guide for Adult Children from Addictive and Other Dysfunctional Families.* San Diego: Recovery Press, 1989.

Napier, Nancy J. *Recreating Your Self: Help for Adult Children of Dysfunctional Families.* New York: Norton, 1991.

Simon, Sidney B., and Suzanne Simon. *Forgiveness: Making Peace with Your Past and Getting on with Your Life.* New York: Warner Books, 1990.

Whitfield, Charles L. *Healing the Child Within.* Deerfield Beach, Fla.: Health Communications, 1987.

Woititz, Janet G. *Adult Children of Alcoholics.* Deerfield Beach, Fla.: Health Communications, 1990.

General Change Strategies

Burns, David D. *Feeling Good: The New Mood Therapy*. New York: Wm. Morrow, 1980.

Freeman, Arthur M., and Rose DeWolfe. *Woulda, Coulda, Shoulda: Overcoming Regrets, Mistakes, and Missed Opportunities*. New York: Wm. Morrow, 1989.

Gawain, Shakti. *Creative Visualization*. New York: Bantam, 1983.

Hay, Louise L. *Heart Thoughts: A Personal Treasury of Inner Wisdom*. Carson, Calif.: Hay House, Inc.

Helmstetter, Shad. *The Self-Talk Solution*. New York: Wm. Morrow, 1987.

Marlin, Emily. *Hope: New Choices and Recovery Strategies for Adult Children of Alcoholics*. New York/San Francisco: HarperCollins, 1988.

Simon, Sidney B. *Getting Unstuck: Breaking Through Your Barriers to Change*. New York: Warner Books, 1989.

Twerski, Abraham J., M.D. *Self-Discovery in Recovery*. Center City, Minn.: Hazelden/Harper, 1984.

Wegscheider-Cruse, Sharon. *Choice-Making for Co-Dependents, Adult Children, and Spirituality Seekers*. Deerfield Beach, Fla.: Health Communications, 1985.

———. *The Miracle of Recovery*. Deerfield Beach, Fla.: Health Communications, 1989.

Dealing with Feelings

Braiker, Harriet B. *Getting Up When You're Feeling Down: A Woman's Guide to Overcoming and Preventing Depression*. New York: G.P. Putnam and Sons, 1988.

Freudenberger, Herbert J., and Gail North. *Situational Anxiety*. New York: Doubleday, 1982.

Goulding, Mary McClure. *Not to Worry! How to Free Yourself from Unnecessary Anxiety and Channel Your Worries into Positive Action*. New York: Silver Arrow (Morrow), 1989.

Lerner, Harriet Goldhor. *Dance of Anger*. New York: HarperCollins, 1989.

Paine-Gernee, Karen, and Terry Hunt, Ed.D. *Emotional Healing: A Program for Emotional Sobriety*. New York: Warner, 1990.

Ulene, Art. *How to Be Angry Without Hurting Anyone*. Random House Books on Phonotape.

Relating to Recover

Alberti, Robert E. *Your Perfect Right: A Guide to Assertive Living.* Inglewood, Calif.: Impact Publishers, 1974.

Bach, Dr. George R., and Peter Wyden. *The Intimate Enemy: How to Fight Fair in Love and Marriage.* New York: Avon, 1968.

Beck, Aaron T. *Love Is Never Enough: How Couples Can Overcome Misunderstandings, Resolve Conflicts, and Solve Relationship Problems Through Cognitive Therapy.* New York: HarperCollins, 1989.

Bower, Sharon Anthony, and Gordon Bower. *Asserting Yourself: A Practical Guide for Positive Change.* Redding, Mass.: Addison-Wesley, 1976.

Earle, Ralph, and Susan Meltsner. *Come Here, Go Away: How to Stop Running From the Love You Want.* New York: Pocket Books, 1991.

Kritsberg, Wayne. *Healing Together: A Guide to Intimacy for Co-dependent Couples.* Deerfield Beach, Fla.: Health Communications, 1989.

Matsakis, Aphrodite. *Compulsive Eaters and Relationships: Ending the Isolation.* Center City, Minn.: Hazelden Educational Materials, 1989.

Paul, Dr. Jordan, and Dr. Margaret Paul. *If You Really Loved Me: From Conflict to Closeness for All Parents and Children.* Minneapolis: CompCare, 1987.

Schaef, Anne Wilson. *Escape from Intimacy: Untangling the "Love" Addictions—Sex, Romance, Relationships.* San Francisco: Harper, 1989.

Smith, Carol Cox. *Recovering Couples: Building Partnerships the Twelve-Step Way.* New York: Bantam, 1992.

Smith, Manuel J. *When I Say No, I Feel Guilty.* Pittsburgh: Bantam, 1985.

Self-Help Index

Index